‖‖ ‖ ‖‖‖‖‖‖‖‖‖‖‖‖‖‖‖‖‖‖‖‖‖‖‖ ‖‖ ‖‖‖

✔ KU-398-653

10|8|22.

SIT
5|16.

Please return on or before the latest date above. 821.
You can renew online at *www.kent.gov.uk/libs* 92
or by telephone 08458 247 200

CUSTOMER SERVICE EXCELLENCE

**Libraries & Archives**

00884\DTP\RN\07.07          LIB 7

C153678433          SIT
ANF

**By the same author:**

*Late Harvest*, Book Guild Publishing, 2003
*Philosophical Explorations Volumes 1–4*, Book Guild Publishing, 2007
*Later Gleanings*, Book Guild Publishing, 2013

821.92

# THE ENTERPRISE OF THE ENGLISH

*An Appreciation of English History in Verse*

S. F. Sharp

Book Guild Publishing

Sussex, England

First published in Great Britain in 2014 by
The Book Guild Ltd
The Werks
45 Church Road
Hove, BN3 2BE

Copyright © S. F. Sharp 2014

The right of S. F. Sharp to be identified as the author of
this work has been asserted by him in accordance with the
Copyright, Designs and Patents Act 1988.

All rights reserved. No part of this publication may be reproduced,
transmitted, or stored in a retrieval system, in any form or by any
means, without permission in writing from the publisher, nor be
otherwise circulated in any form of binding or cover other than that
in which it is published and without a similar condition being
imposed on the subsequent purchaser.

Typesetting in Bembo by
Keyboard Services, Luton, Bedfordshire

Printed in Great Britain by
CPI Group (UK) Ltd, Croydon, CR0 4YY

A catalogue record for this book is available from
The British Library.

ISBN 978 1 909716 87 2

*Dedicated to my brother Victor and sister June,
and my late brother Peter John*

# Introduction

The history of England is a fascinating record of great enterprise. A small island off the coast of Europe by its own efforts became the greatest empire the world has ever known. It also became the originator of social, technical, manufacturing and financial innovations that have transformed the world – a remarkable series of achievements.

In this poem I have tried to describe the broad sweep of this great enterprise in relatively simple language, because of my strong belief that the foremost function of language is to communicate. Obscure allusions or baroque sentences often only detract from understanding. At the same time, to keep up the pace of this dynamic endeavour, I have had to deal with great events and interesting personalities very briefly. This leaves it open for readers who are interested to make further enquiries about the persons and events all too fleetingly mentioned.

Putting history into rhymed verse is not easy, for many names of persons and places do not always lend themselves readily to an adopted metre. There is a further difficulty: I personally prefer short poems which can be honed like beautiful gems. A short poem has been described as a 'picture in beautiful words', but an epic is more like a large tapestry of many narrative pictures woven in poetic words against a backcloth of less striking material. It is inevitable that not every part of an epic will be arresting or of equal interest.

As to why I should have attempted to write this epic, I cannot really answer. Why does an artist paint his pictures? Why does a sculptor shape his sculptures? Why does a composer create his music? There was an overriding impulse to write verse (as well as philosophical essays) which seemed the most natural thing to do, partly out of interest, but principally a kind of self-expression that could not be denied.

Moreover, I obtained immense pleasure from writing this epic even though it involved much hard intellectual and physical work. Fitting plain events into verse is akin to solving non-cryptic crossword puzzles but more satisfying and more sublime because, to be successful, it must be invested with genuine feeling. A further advantage for me was that writing verse has always been a pleasant contrast to the more rigorous writing of philosophy.

I would have liked to continue working on and improving this epic, but increasing age – at eighty – is against me. Whatever its merits or demerits, it is the best I can do. I have worked on it, on and off, for over twenty years and feel now is the time to publish, or never.

By keeping the language straightforward, I hope this poem will also be read by young people who, I feel, ought to know what we as a nation have achieved, aided ably by the Scots, the Welsh and the Irish. Above all, I hope it will inspire them to achieve even greater things in the future. Our story does not, and should not, end with the passing of the empire. Our native genius remains as alive today as ever it was in the past.

S. F. Sharp, Milton Regis, Kent

# The Enterprise of the English

*Upon the cliffs of Dover, looking out to sea,*
*An ancient scholar once addressed these words to me:*
Look yonder at the foaming sea and at this sky.
What does it mean to you? *he asked me with a sigh.*
What does it mean to you, the future of our race?
What means this little isle set down in this fair place?
*Before my answer could be made he spoke again.*
*This time his voice was thick and full of fatal pain.*
Just sit a while with me and listen to my tale.
I must relate it now before my strength shall fail.
I must pass on the spirit of our fathers' fame,
That you might bear the torch and keep alive our flame.
This little island set amidst the seething sea
Invites the roving ships to harbour in its lea,
To shelter from the storms and camp upon its shore,
Or track its pathless ways, the valleys to explore.
Throughout the ages there came a flood of homeless men
And wave on wave they came, they stayed, then left again.
No trace they left; a silent tide that ebbed and flowed
Against the formless mass of those who wore the woad.
Ah, look beyond the mists of time. Do you not see
The Iron folk who came across an arid sea?
Before the waters rose and formed the channel deep
That serves both as a sore constraint and fortress keep.
Much later came the Roman legions' noble ranks:
Almighty Caesar trod upon these rolling banks.
He too looked out to sea towards his native land,
Shielding his eyes as you do now with level hand.
But he was looking back, whilst you must look before.
He was arriving here, whilst you must leave the shore.

1

All England soon beneath the Roman law and road
Became enslaved, except the wearers of the woad.
They fled before the iron shield and bloody sword:
Wild from the mountain heights they shrieked and roared,
Descending oft to steal, to slay their foreign foes,
Only to fade away before the Romans rose.
So Hadrian built his wall and fortified its length,
'Gainst which the angry Celts might waste their naked strength.
Three hundred years of troubled peace the Romans gave,
But Britons never would endure the role of slave.
Where'er they looked they saw the boundless sea and sky.
They fought to be free, nor were afraid to die:
Better a free man dead than live a life in chains.
Who loses all wins all, if he but freedom gains.
But Roman hearts were not for long on England set.
They looked across the seas to Rome, began to fret,
To feel the warm Italian sun and taste sweet wine:
Oh, how for distant homes these sons of Mars did pine.
At length those calls of warmer climes and home did win,
So with the Dark Ages, like storm clouds, closing in,
The Roman occupation ceased to hold its own
And England had to look to its defence alone.

*The scholar paused a while and shook his ancient head.*
Not all who came were evil men, *he quietly said.*
St Patrick came to Ireland his mission to begin,
To teach the love of God and save us from our sin.
Yet all this time from England came an awful groan,
Appealing far too late for help from distant Rome.

# King Arthur

Whilst from the west King Arthur's men advancing came,
That strong and noble king of roundéd table fame,
Who fought the hostile hordes until his tragic death.
When wounded lay and with his weak and dying breath,
Three times he begged Sir Lancelot his sword to sink
Beneath the lake: at each request that knight would shrink,
Until at last he threw the mighty sword on high
And watched its jewelled blade go soaring through the sky.
But just before it hit the waters of the mere,
A white and slender hand did from the depths appear
To grasp the hilt about and make of circles three,
Then drew the kingly sword beneath that inland sea.
With Arthur dead, how could the Saxon plan succeed?
Across the fields of death their bodies lay like weeds.
Though dark these sad and savage times may seem to be,
A Christian light came gleaming across the restless sea:
Augustine lands in Kent to preach the holy word;
By many were his peaceful words most welcome heard,
And in the north Oswald, a Celtic Christian king,
At Heavenfield victorious arms and hearts did bring.
Alas, Northumbrian might would not for long prevail:
At Nectansmere its dream of dominance would fail.
But just before that time the Whitby Synod made
The Roman Christ prevail, and let the Celtic fade.
Note well that round the darkest cloud shall light appear:
He who believes in good shall never more know fear.
Thus England, in these troubled hours, she stood alone,
Pursued the love of Good and made it for her own.
Now came the Viking ships to raid our luckless land
With hornéd helmets, shields and savage swords in hand.

At first the Mercian king, then Wessex took to sword,
But later they bowed low before a Danish lord.


## King Alfred

Before that time King Alfred burned the unwatched cakes:
When dreams of England's might his concentration breaks,
He broods before the fire and stares within its flame
And dreams his pleasant dream of England's future fame.
Such are the dreams from which our future times are spun,
It took him many years before he battles won.
He built a navy strong that guarded well the sea
And from the Danish ships he kept his domain free.
He fortified the land and trained his armies bold,
Nor, wisely, would he purchase peace with Danish gold.
He made just laws and ruled an England strong,
He cultivated prose and minstrels' lilting song,
And to the English court the scholars came once more
To keep alive the sacred flame of ancient lore.
But when in death he lay within his warrior grave,
No one this lovely land from Viking raids could save.
And in their wake more Danish kings did briefly stay,
But no one could now the Norman flood of arms allay.


## Canute

As if prophetic of his future doom, Canute
Could not the rising of the restless tide refute.
However great or strong a kingly will may be,
No mortal man could e'er hold back the ceaseless sea,
Nor forces greater than those he can command.

To yield or perish is hard nature's harsh demand,
But man forever fights and will not cease to try:
Oh, never let his dauntless spirit fade and die.
It is the crown of folly, yet it nobly breeds,
And from this spirit spring a thousand fertile seeds,
And all the while the English spirit quietly drew
That simple wisdom which is lost except to few.
The will of man, though strong and brave, can never defeat
The forces of natural law, but must at first retreat
Until by thought he can the force of nature bend,
Which as it goes untamed serves nonetheless his end.
Canute could not command the rising tide to stay,
Nor could the Norman tide for long be kept at bay.


## William I

King Harold lost his life and England found fresh shame
As Norman knights rode in, this pleasant land to claim.
They had compiled a list of all the wealth they took
And set it down for us to read in Domesday Book.
How great is human folly that believes it can
Enslave the mind and carefree heart of any man.
No one possesses what he takes: in acts of greed
Sown are the seed that will, in time, destroy the deed.
These Norman lords came not to sack and loot the land,
But gave it out amongst their proud conquering band,
That they might settle here and reap the harvest seed
And cause this fertile land to supply their every need.
The conquered serfs were set to work their masters' soil
And yield a part of the rich fruit of their hard toil.
Each Norman lord had built his sturdy fortress keep,
That midst a hostile folk he might untroubled sleep.

Such castles made the land secure, and fitful peace
Came to these troubled isles as most invasions cease.
How sweet the pause that comes amidst protracted strife!
How calm the moment's rest we snatch from fevered life!
Absorbing all the nobler features of our race,
The Norman knights infused their energetic pace.
Most loyal fiefs to kings they proved themselves to be,
Embraced the Christian faith with sober expectancy,
Encouraging great monasteries and scholar bands
To spread their gentler spirit far throughout these lands.
One man above all others left his peerless mark
Upon this island people still confused and dark.
A bastard born, he fought against his shameful fate
To earn by his own efforts alone the title 'Great'.
He learned to master difficulties one by one
And never gave up hope until his will was done.
He had a breadth of aim and patient statesmanship
That never once allowed his firm control to slip,
But most of all he had a strong and stubborn will
That learned to make advantage of persistent ill,
Whilst deep within, the sea-wolves' fiery blood fierce ran
And made his savage spirit strong – a wrathful man!
Though good, yet he could seek revenge most ruthlessly,
That his great frame and fearsome face with furiosity
Would tremble like the raging of a savage beast
Against the petty confines of unwanted leash.
William the Conqueror became our robust king,
Of whose exploits and laws the minstrels rightly sing.
He treated with moderation fair the Saxon horde,
But was not slow to rule with deathly, heartless sword,
As when, returning home from nearby Normandy,
He quelled the efforts of the Saxons to be free:
Put down rebellions in the west, preserved his line;

6

Laid waste this restless country from the Humber to the
  Tyne;
Laid siege to Hereward the Wake on Ely's Isle,
With shallow boats a causeway made, such was his guile,
Until the camp of refuge fell into his hands
And he regained control of these wild fen lands.
King William the feudal system perfect made,
Enacted game and forest laws, encouraged trade
And introduced the nightly village curfew bell
That signalled clear, 'Put out your fire and sleep ye well!'
(In England's timbered homes the wayward spark could fire
And turn a sleeping house into a flaming pyre.)
Alas, his closing years by wilful sons were cursed,
When in old Normandy by Robert he was worsed:
Engaged in single combat, William was sore hurt
As from his gallant horse he fell to bite the dirt.
How harsh is just fate that makes our brood as bad
As we that bred these curs! Oh, nothing is so sad
As foul ingratitude that bites the hand that feeds,
When sons betray their sires in all their words and deeds.


**Red Rufus**

At last Great William died; Red Rufus took his throne,
A selfish, greedy man who made this land his own:
Oppressed the clergy, then extorted gold from all,
Yet proudly rushed to fight at Hermit Peter's call.
From every part of Europe noble princes came,
Both kings and peasants, side by side, with faith aflame.
Each wore the cross of red upon the cloth of white
Against the crescent of the Turks in Christian fight.
This first Crusade set out Jerusalem to free:

7

Except for one brief spell, this dream was not to be.
When hunting in the New Forest, Rufus was slain,
His was, alas, by many judged a worthless reign.
Although unloved, some good came from what he did:
He built a bridge across the Thames, and likewise hid
The fortress tower by a stone encircling wall,
And built in stately style Westminster's famous hall.


## Henry I

Henry I took up the stately crown of gold,
Forestalling brother Robert's claim to have and hold.
How often absence makes or mars the lot of man
Who, having missed but once his chance, an 'also-ran'
Remains until the end of these historic days.
How oft is fate unmade by untoward delays
And fortunes astutely made by actions swift and sure!
Henry's charter of liberties relieved the poor.
He too restored the good old laws which Rufus broke
And lifted thus oppression's dull, unyielding yoke.
So when the elder Robert reached this wanted realm,
He found the younger Henry accepted at its helm.
Henry, Matilda married – she, a Saxon bride,
Could trace her noble line to Edmund Ironside.
She was a daughter of Malcolm the Scottish king;
Her mother was the sister of Edgar Atheling.
Norman and Saxon lines Henry this way unites,
And so reduces just cause for bitter civil fights.
At Tenchebrai defeats; chains up in Cardiff's keep
The luckless Robert. Free-roaming mountain sheep
In peaceful ease and free of anxious haunting fears
Crop by the castle where for twenty-eight long years
This royal prince a prisoner's dull routine led,

Nor won his freedom 'til the day he was found dead.
William, the son of Robert, fair Normandy claimed
Until defeated at Brenville, but was not yet tamed.
So tries once more; this time in battle he was killed.
So much rich noble blood for earthly gain is spilled:
Would that as much for higher and better things been bled,
Then we poor mortals might be proud of countless dead.
Ironic fate now plays its hand, offsetting Henry's gain,
For drowns his son at sea: 'He never smiled again.'
A drunken crew had brought the king this bitter grief
When they let run the white ship on the deadly reef.
Blame not those others, foolish king, but look within:
Thy fate is but the just reward for thine own sin.
He who would gain this earthly world entire and whole
Gains nothing in the end and loses all, his soul!
The loss of only sons to kings is doubly sad,
For one fell blow destroys all hopes they ever had
Of passing on their throne to son as noble heir:
The very thing they prized the most adds to despair.
Henry summoned his barons to Windsor Castle's keep
To swear his daughter to support when death's long sleep
Caused him to lie in silent grave. Matilda queen?
The barons let the king believe in years between,
But when he died and Stephen snatched the royal crown,
These self-same nobles let him and Matilda down,
Preferring to be led in council and in war
Not by a woman frail, but by a man of gore.


**Stephen I**

For Stephen was a valiant warrior of renown,
Extremely popular in all the shires around.
When Normandy followed the English barons' lead,

Matilda's husband Geoffrey, with commendable speed,
Reduced them to submission and retained that land,
Refusing to allow it to fall in the usurper's hand.
King Stephen, to retain his barons' strong support,
Danegeld abolished and allowed the barons' sport
Of hunting freely their own forests wild and deep.
He built new castles, each with its sturdy keep,
From which these robber barons sallied forth with arms,
Holding to ransom all, creating great alarms
By their barbaric treatment of the men they seized,
Doing with them whate'er they evilly chose or pleased.
A time of troubles, of civil, most wretched war
Without the just and firm restraint of regal law.
His weak title made Stephen concessions give
If he upon his stolen throne would safely live.
Oh, most injudicious king, who thought he could thus buy
Allegiance of unscrupulous barons who'd try
To take advantage of the gifts he freely gave
While all the time they played the unrestrainéd knave.
He was not bad, but lacked the firm and iron will
That could alone bring these unruly men to heel.
The guilty often see themselves in other men
And fear the tricks they played will back on them soon bend.
So powerful Roger, Bishop of Salisbury's Plain,
King Stephen snatched – imprisoned him with ball and chain
And stole his rich estate – because he feared that man,
Enraging thus the church, and turned his brother's hand
Against the king, to turn on Matilda's rightful side.
A king who'd tigers mount needs must those tigers ride!
Now came more troubles, thick and fast, as Scotland's king,
Espousing his niece's cause, his armies fling
Across the border's dividing line, invading England
Only to meet defeat by Thurstan's martial band.

A cross and flag the English upon a wagon pulled,
Thus 'Battle of the Standard' was this conflict called.
The tides of civil war now swiftly ebb and flow:
At Lincoln, Stephen captured, seemed to be brought low,
But then Robert was by a royal army snatched,
For whom Stephen in exchange was soon despatched.
Why fickle fate ordained that these events should be,
And neither prisoner slain, that both might soon be free,
Is difficult for us to rightly comprehend.
The wily ways of fate and fortune lie beyond our ken:
Sometimes we think that man alone his fortune makes,
Until events overwhelm and fate his fortune breaks.
Had Stephen died, how different would have been our lot,
For England then might well be ruled over by a Scot!
When Robert died, Matilda to Normandy returned,
Although her heart upon the throne of England yearned.
In time her son, another Henry, revived her cause:
The king on stolen throne enjoys no let nor pause!
Henry was master of Normandy and Aquitaine
And sought the crown of England for himself to gain.
'Twas then that fate delivers its oft-repeated trick
That cuts the too-ambitious king unto the quick.
For Stephen's son now died and left the throne no heir:
Imagine if you can the king's outraged despair!
So by a treaty made at Winchester he swore
That Henry would become the king, avoiding war,
Whilst keeping England's throne within the family's keep
When Stephen came, like all, to sleep the eternal sleep.

## Henry II

And so it came to be that Henry took the throne.
He ruled one-third of France, and ruled alone.

How fared the common folk during these bitter days?
They were oppressed and made to act in servile ways.
The gap between the ruler and the ruled grew wide,
With different tongue in use on either hostile side.
Yet note that trade and commerce, art and science grew,
Illuminated scrolls and churchly music too,
Whilst broad square towers and round-arched churches stand
This very day in many towns throughout our land:
A legacy of days when, under Norman rule,
The conqueror held power from his fortress hall.
These Normans brought a love of gardens cool and fair,
Whose fertile blossoms filled the balmy evening air.
They added to the Saxon tongue their own rich speech
And courtly modes and styles the plainer Saxons teach.
Our race has risen by its gift to keep the best
Of those it met and let oblivion take the rest.
With common sense it ne'er condemns a foreign style
Because it is a stranger way, but all the while
Takes note to glean if better it should prove to be
And then adopts the very best enthusiastically.
A people slow to change or to give up the old
And trusted ways that proved their weight in living gold,
But quick to seize the better ways to make their own,
Whatever fate upon these shores as flotsam blown.
Henry Plantagenet soon curbed the barons' might
By razing castle keeps; restored the rule of right,
Thus stopped their robbery and violent misrule
With ever-ready sword and judgement firm and cool.
This youthful king, whose fathers wore the humble broom,★
With wisdom sought to make this sorry island bloom,

---

★The name Plantagenet is from *planta genista*, the Latin name for broom, a sprig of which the first Count of Anjou used to wear in his helmet in the Holy Land as an emblem of humility.

But like so many men who grasp at power's sun,
He thought that he alone should be the only one:
Alone should make decree and justice freely give,
Through him alone should all have cause to die or live.
As favourite companion of this youthful king,
Thomas à Becket was made gift of everything.
When he was made chancellor of this fair isle,
He lived and dined in rich and rather lavish style.
But when to suit the king's desire to rule the church
He occupied Archbishop Canterbury's perch,
Belated Becket now found the spirit to deny
His king's long wish to rule the church and priests to try
By royal judges instead of by a church-filled court:
To this edict he would not give his full support.
'Appoint no prelates' so another edict went;
'Appoint no prelates more' without the king's consent.
Small wonder Thomas seemed ungrateful to his friend
When to such rules as these he could not, would not bend.
'Have I not raised this stubborn man to high estate,
Who, churlish, dares my royal will to so frustrate?'
When friends fall out, what bitterness and spite holds sway:
We hate those most who most we loved, who now betray.
So Thomas fled to France beyond the angry reach
Of his determined king, who might in wrath impeach
A will that was opposed to what he wished to see.
For six long years the exile kept from England free,
Until the king repented, in hope that Thomas would
Be more amenable to see what's to his good.
But Becket proved much firmer now than ere he went,
Nor once his moral opposition would repent.
'Will no one rid me of this proud, ungrateful priest?'
The king in anger roused the dark avenging beast
That lay within the breasts of four most loyal knights,

13

Who took it on themselves to put these things to rights.
Imagine if you can! Oh, foul unholy scene
That was in Canterbury's cathedral soon seen
When Thomas, kneeling down his prayers to say,
Refusing still to flee nor yet his church betray,
Saw round about him crowd with swords of angry steel
The loyal knights who would enforce their master's will.
'Most stubborn priest, possessed of otherworldly might,
Consider that you may be wrong and Henry right:
And soon, as royal favourite restored again,
What happy honours more might you not yet attain!'
Alas, the man who will not yield his fate defies:
There is no peace for him unless, until, he dies.
Those bloodied swords the house of God with murder
    taint,
And slayed the man – but made the martyred priest a saint.
From every part of Europe wend the pilgrim throng
To view the spot on which was done this grievous wrong.
Too late, King Henry wished his lips had never said
Those fateful words that to this dreadful murder led.
For Thomas once, was still, a friend whose loss he grieved,
Who differed from his king in what he firm believed.
This noble king in penitence, from guilt would crave
The monks to scourge his abject flesh by Becket's grave.
Only the strongest men know when to bend most low,
That they in stature might before their subjects grow!
Meanwhile, in answer to deposéd Dermot's plea,
The king allowed Richard de Clare to cross the sea
And land his knights on Ireland's wild and troubled shore,
Ostensibly to bring that realm within his law.
For 'Lord of Ireland' by papal bull was Henry styled,
But by Strongbow's rapid prowess became most riled,
Fearing lest Strongbow would soon claim to be a king

(Ambitions grow when all around your praises sing!)
Especially as de Clare had won vast lands and power,
While Henry desired to leave England, whose glower
Of indignation grew most dark at Becket's death.
On absent men people waste not their censorious breath:
Most crimes are oft the censure of the passing hour
Which soon the appetite for novelty will devour.
'Tis best when troubles loom to lure the watching eyes
With deeds elsewhere to take all 'look-outs' by surprise.
So Henry landed on Ireland's green and fertile shore,
Received submission from the kings without a war,
As Strongbow had already won on battlefield
Enough to force most of the Irish kings to yield.
Although, except within the well-armed 'English Pale',
The English rule of Ireland proved but nominal.
Ah me! What sad, sad times are these when sons rebel:
Their treachery one is ashamed to speak or tell.
Urged on by mother's pleas and with King Louis' aid,
And helped by William, king of Scotland, so they made
An unsuccessful bid to strike King Henry down.
But Henry fought them off at Alnwick, nor gave ground,
Imprisoned William – 'The Lion' – for his iniquity
And forced the king of Scotland to swear he'd vassal be
To him and him alone. He further made it known
This victory must by heaven be condoned
And he forgiven by the power in the sky
For any part he played in letting Becket die.
A clever, cunning move! Oh thou true soldier king
Who turns to his advantage thus that wicked thing!
He was at heart a man of peace who made good laws,
But nonetheless was not averse to show his claws.
Within his reign the circuit judges and the assizes
Became the courts from which the common law arises,

15

While payment of a scutage tax made weaker yet
The feudal system which, some say, we would regret.
The dying days of Henry embittered by the strife
Of sons' rebellions broke his heart, cut short his life.
Too oft in history's dark chronicles it is seen
Ambition breaks a family's trust and comes between
A father and his son or other distant kin:
For want of a throne, heirs wade through a sea of sin.

## Richard I

Brave Richard Coeur de Lion became our absent king,
A man who could accomplish all or anything.
Oh, valiant crusader, poet of renown,
Most gallant hero of romance to wear our crown,
(Alas, 'tis little use to be all these when far,
Chasing the fond illusion of a distant star!)
Rich London Jews offered you their gold to aid
The speedy, well-armed launching of the third Crusade.
Ungracious king, you had them rudely chased away,
Which fed the rumour that Jews were fair game to slay.
And hideous mobs broke down their doors that they might kill
The owners of the treasures they came to steal.
Oh, what foul blot is this when in their frenzy the mob
Do loot and kill, and kill and loot, the Jews to rob!
In northern York, to its eternal, lasting shame,
No hope of mercy caused the Jews to put themselves to
    flame
In castle's refuge to which from rabid mobs they fled.
Imagine if you can their agony and dread!
All those who occupy the highest office should
Take care to guard their acts, say only what is good,

Lest hasty men, ambitious for a patron's praise,
Should seize upon each thoughtless deed or careless phrase
And do what they believe will please their master's whim –
Then, should they do much wrong, will blame it all on him!
King Richard sold such lands and offices of state
As would his high crusading aims perpetuate:
Royal charters sold he to eager wealthy towns
Until his treasure chest with fighting gold abounds.
With Philip, king of France, from Vézelai they sail –
One hundred thousand men must weather out the gale
On Sicily's convenient isle; King Richard's bride-
To-be Berengaria now sailed to join his side.
At last the splendid fleet set out from Messina's port,
The kings excited and eager for their martial sport,
With flags and standards held aloft for all to see
The noble might of this most gallant armoury.
But fate, who eyes the petty games of foolish men
With malicious mischief, intervened yet once again
And cast shipwrecked on Cyprus's coast King Richard's 'wife',
Whose pursuit by cruel Isaac put at risk her life.
For he, inhuman tyrant, the dread of pilgrim bands,
The scourge of shipwrecked men who fell into his hands,
Would capture her with Joan, the sister of the king,
Had not good Richard come to stop this evil thing.
He soon deposed Bad Isaac and assumed the Cyprus throne,
And married fair Berengaria, made her his own.
The Christian kings arrived in Palestine at last,
Taking the port of Acre in which their ships made fast.
They went to fight their way through Saladin's fierce force
And snatch Jerusalem by dint of armed resource.
Heroic Richard swung his mighty battleaxe
And cut his way right through in spite of fresh attacks.
Each step of the one hundred miles he bravely fought,

From Acre to Ascalon, to such renowned report
That Philip, king of France, jealous of his fame,
In pique returned to France to hide his bitter shame.
Alas, the lack of money and much allied dissent
Made Richard sign a treaty with his opponent.
In pilgrim's dress disguised, Richard when homeward bound,
Was foolishly betrayed on foreign hostile ground
When his imprudent page wore gloves, the mark of rank,
To buy provisions in. For this he had to thank
His capture by the Duke of Austria, whom he'd struck:
Such is the back returning flight of fate or luck!
Once do a wrong and it will hunt throughout the years
And seek you out in spite of all your bitter tears.
The man you struck and then forgot appears once more
When you are down, to grind you deeper to the floor.
This duke sold Richard to Henry, the German king,
Who deep into his Tyrol castle keep did fling
The hapless warrior bold. Such is the curse of fame
That puts a heavy ransom price on well-known name!
To seek out where his king was hid, a minstrel gay
From castle keep to castle keep sweet sung a lay
Which was composed by Richard long years before,
Until he heard an answering beyond the door
That kept the world outside the Tyrol castle wall.
Thus Blondel heard the king's rich-toned answering call,
Then for a heavy ransom sum Richard was freed,
At last to make his way to England with all speed.
For meanwhile John had tried to seize his brother's crown –
Encouraged by Philip of France, whom Richard had put
    down,
To gratify his wounded pride – but 'twas in vain,
For Richard, home, continued well his noble reign,
And John's foul treason and his base ingratitude

He pardoned, and with regal solicitude,
By making John his heir instead of Geoffrey's son.
(The times they were too troubled for so young a one.)
At Gisors Richard defeated the scheming king of France
Who once too oft against our king his arms did chance.
Alas, next year on Richard fell a fatal blow
That was to bring this lion-hearted man so low.
Though he forgave the archer whose arrow had strayed,
The hapless man by loyal friends alive was flayed.
So ended not as it might a noble, gallant reign.
Alas, we shall but seldom see his like again.
During his absent reign there lived bold Robin Hood
Who, with his merry outlawed men, lived in deep Sherwood
And stole from all the rich and foreign knights
To give unto the poor, uphold their ancient rights.
He swore to keep the throne for Richard's glad return,
For which all those oppressed by John so longingly yearn.
Momentous was the flowering of Richard's reign,
Though his long absence cause his subjects pain.
Much good was done by founding courts of common pleas
And courts of admiralty that would command the seas,
While crests resplendent were first used to deck the shields
And leopards three passant the king of England wields.
Such things add to the glory of the fighting king:
Throughout the halls of history his fame will ring!


## John

The crown of England rests on John's uneasy head:
At once to France he goes to quell rebellions led
By Arthur, Duke of Brittany, whose claims
As son of John's own elder brother all France proclaims.

King John his nephew snatched and drowned him in the
    Seine,
Nor would, to answer for this crime, in France remain,
Though summoned by its king to come before his court.
So all his French domains by this ill-timed default
Were doomed to be forfeited − lost for good
Those lands o'er which the flag of England long had stood.
Seek not to get nor keep by evil's wicked means,
Lest natural justice likewise badly intervenes
To rob unscrupulous cheats of what they sought to gain:
Was not Lackland's own honour drownéd in the Seine?
When Canterbury's archbishop gave up his life
It soon became the cause of further bitter strife.
Pope Innocent declared that Stephen Langton should
Take up his predecessor's staff for holy good.
But John saw this a violation of his rights as king,
Not his own choice but a humiliating thing.
He would not let this Langton act as Rome ordained;
The Pope in turn had now the rebel king restrained:
All England under a dire interdict he placed,
And no more religious ceremonies our churches graced.
The people, their customary holy ceremonies gone,
In awesome fear of everlasting hell did mourn.
The churches even closed their 'ever-open' doors
And priests ceased all their functions, by holy laws
No sacraments administered, whilst o'er the dead
No last comforting prayers were now quietly said
And they, in poor unconsecrated ground were laid,
Nor were the chimes of village church bells sweet played.
How mournful falls the shadow of this interdict −
A nation punished by a popish rule so strict:
'Why punish us so much for this, the king's own crime?'
The Pope reversed this injustice in good time:

His bull of excommunication on the king,
With threats to give the crown to France, repentance
  brings.
King John gave England as the fief of Holy See,
For which he paid a thousand marks as tribute fee.
This tyrant's harsh extortions riled his barons so
That Norman lords and English plot to bring him low.
Most bad, ignoble king! The common foes unite,
Antagonistic factions forgo their fight
And like as brothers link their armies into one:
Thus out of evil deeds has lasting goodness come!
These barons forced the king to sign the Magna Carta
And for fair England's freedom swore in formal barter
On which the future greatness of this country lay:
Let all who love this isle remember well that day!
To men of treachery such oaths are meaningless,
For John recruited foreign armies to impress
Upon the rebel barons his own selfish will,
Thus causing civil war – a bitter, lasting ill.
He turned the swords of noble men against their own:
What wickedness issued from England's evil throne!
In desperation turned the barons to fair France,
Enlisted the aid of Louis, who grasped this proffered chance
Upon our throne to sit and rule this troubled isle.
Yet Louis proved too weak and full of Gallic guile.
In such joint ventures all should get an equal share,
But Louis' preference showed: he used our knights unfair.
Though the modern man may scorn that gods should
  intervene
In sad affairs of man, some law is plainly seen
Which visits retribution upon his evil child:
When John's army traversed The Wash, the weather wild
Whipped up and sank the royal boats and treasure ships,

And under deep and whirling waves John's baggage slips –
An omen, if you like, that his unwholesome ride
Was soon to be swept out on fate's remorseless tide.
Like one condemned, King John with food and wine hid
   grief.
In the excess of peach and ale he found no relief:
A fever broke its clammy beads upon his brow
And all his sinful life ebbed slowly from him now.
The king was dead. No nation mourned. No church more
   glad.
His crown was passed to Henry, Third, who was just a lad:
A boy of comely grace and charm, of winters ten,
How could he rule an island full of angry men?
Before we close the book on John's most wretched reign,
Let's balance out the loss with what England did gain.
We lost the provinces of France, except for two –
Guienne and Gascony remained. No one need rue
Such loss which made our king pay greater heed to home
Instead of e'er on French wars to distant roam.
And in John's reign the London Bridge was built complete
As rich and prosperous became our fishing fleet.
And London Town each year a mayor first elects,
With sheriffs twain: her best the City proud selects.
Alas, the persecution of the wretched Jew
Is not abated by those splendid measures new.
But with Christian charity let's wish the poor king well:
May some redeeming deed keep him from Satan's hell!


### Henry III

Now by the Pope's decree Henry III was king,  .
A boy of tender years, a weak, defenceless thing

O'er whom the Earl of Pembroke wielded protective rule:
An old and prudent statesman, he was no man's fool.
When French Louis besieged fair Lincoln's castle keep,
The old protector proved that he was not asleep:
Defeated the French in treacherous Dover's narrow seas;
The French fleet broke, before Hubert de Burgh soon
    swiftly flees
(This cunning sailor sailed to windward side apace,
To throw the burning quicklime onto the Frenchmen's face!)
Louis conceded defeat and left fierce England's shore.
Now free of foreign foes and free from civil war,
This land for just a span obtained welcome release
As times of troubled strife and arméd conflicts cease.
Though hordes of foreign mercenaries roamed the land,
They did not form one single threat'ning warring band.
Henry, alas, when he became a man, betrayed
The trust and hope for which his people long had prayed.
Weak-minded, selfish and tyrannical, he governed ill,
His court with foreign favourites proceeds to fill.
He took Eleanor of Provence to be his wife,
Whose gay and wealthy friends became a cause of strife.
Provincial courtiers were the favourites of the king
And to these shores their shining genius did bring.
Among these men, Simon de Montfort, noble knight,
Well served the native folk, prepared for them to fight
And keep the fragile flame of liberty alive.
Against the powers of the king he'd bravely strive,
Who'd headstrong grown – until this knight at Oxford led
The armed and angry barons, who placed him at their head.
Captured the king, and caused a parliament to sit,
Drew up demands and bade the king abide by it.
'Mad parliament' though latterly 'twas called, and yet
We owe this first assembly much, let's not forget!

23

These barons called four knights from each county to voice
Each district's grievances, and by their own free choice
A sheriff would be elected by votes concise and clear,
And parliament would meet three times in every year;
Whilst last but not the least, public accounts be kept,
A chore for which past kings had proved not well adept!
Henry, as soon as he obtained his freedom, swore
He would not keep his word and what is, sadly, more,
He tried by forceful means to gain that power lost
And England once again in civil war was tossed.
The barons took up arms and under Simon's lead
Defeated the king at Lewes, who must all powers concede.
Prince Edward was handed o'er as hostage for the king
And Simon seized control: loud did the church bells ring!
So Simon wisely ruled, and parliament reforms
Which represented all: a lull before dark storms!
For Edward, princely hostage for the foolish king,
Escaped his guards and into battle his forces fling.
At Evesham's fertile vale Simon de Montfort was slain:
The barons' cause must fail until they rise again.
Oh, fickle twists of fate which rob the good of life
Before they have the chance to settle bitter strife!
What wariness effective is when fates intrude?
By placing Henry first, which Simon had thought shrewd,
Rebounds as the armies clashed together in the fray.
To save his life the king did loudly, clearly say:
'I am Henry of Winchester, kill not your king!'
And so he lived, this weak-minded, and selfish thing.
De Montfort's earldom and his rich estates
To Crouchback given are, so history relates:
The second son whose house of Lancaster shall rise,
Resplendent powerful before men's watchful eyes.
And when Edward ascends the royal throne, then war

24

Which split this noble realm divides the land no more.
Too soon our prince set sail to join the sixth Crusade
With many barons bold in battledress arrayed.
With him went too his wife, Eleanor, sweet and brave,
Who sucked his poison wound, his very life to save.
A dagger wound turned foul, his kingly life might kill,
Had not his wife with loving lips his wound made heal.
Amid the horrors of history's sorry plight,
Such selfless deeds as this shine forth their hopeful light.
Of man's oft wicked ways we need not full despair
When every now and then is born someone to care.
A common ploy of kings when homelands draw the sword
To look elsewhere and wage a worthwhile war abroad.
So when King Henry died, Prince Edward was acclaimed:
Why should a loyal son for a father's faults be blamed?
Encloséd forests were opened in Henry's reign,
No more did breaches of their laws mean death's last pain.
Many a beautiful church and tall cathedral spires
Were built to grace the growing towns and wealthy shires.
Westminster Abbey was rebuilt – most noble shrine,
Whose sacred ground receives the finest of our line.


## Edward I

Edward I, with great ambition, dared to be
The monarch of these isles entire from sea to sea.
He wanted wild Wales and Scotland's steep and rugged land
To fall within the grasp of his firm royal hand.
At first from Llewellyn demands homage pay
And grew incensed when the Welsh king kept well away.
Invaded the verdant valleys of sweet-water'd Wales,
Until the lesser might of poor Llewellyn fails.

Then swiftly marches on, the north of Wales to win:
Llewellyn slain, all Wales is taken completely in.
King Edward swore to leaders of the Welsh to give
A prince born in their land to rule and there to live,
Who spoke no word of English, nor of French at all,
Which pleased them well: but soon his promise would appal
When he his infant son as Prince of Wales proclaimed
And made these cheated knights bend low, disgraced, ashamed.
Soon all wild Wales, annexed to England, lost its voice
And joined by force our destiny with little choice.
Before Edward on Scotland turned his avid eye,
Twelve years of troubled peace, uneasy peace, went by.
Then he was asked to state on whom succession falls
When Scottish kings could not decide which of them
    rules.
How oft disputing kings call in a foreign power
Which then proceeds the both of them to swift devour!
Edward demands they pay him homage as of yore:
They'd paid such homage to our English kings before.
Had not the Scottish Lion, William, to his shame,
Become sworn vassal of our kings, betrayed his name?
What gifts will not a king bestow when he's defeated,
For life is sweet and never more may be repeated!
Richard I, 'tis true, released the Scots for gold,
But this old waiver should not for his successors hold.
A king has no right to sell, it seems, though they might bind
Their subjects vassal to another's rule, we find.
What logic lies in this? How can they both be true?
Do kings possess a logic rare, known but to few?
Alas, no logic guides the fates of royal crown,
Except when two contend, the weaker bows him down!
The only right is might, that is hard nature's law,
Enforced by beasts of prey, blood-red in tooth and claw.

('Tis not all gloom, all dark and dismal dank despair,
For natural justice soon will every loss repair.)
From thirteen claimants to the vacant Scottish throne,
Edward appoints John Balliol as the king alone.
But soon King John grew tired of this tight vassal yoke
And all allegiance to the English crown he broke.
Defeat at Dunbar won the English Scotland's throne
And so to London came the famous Stone of Scone,
On which all Scottish kings were crowned with solemn rite.
And so was joined fierce Scotland's pride to English might,
Though Wallace tried to free the fallen Scots, he fell
And from a scaffold swung, a brave but silenced bell.
Edward 'the English Justinian' was rightly styled
As he our ancient laws judiciously conciled,
And in his reign he well established parliament.
No more could kings raise money's worth without consent.
The jurisdiction of the courts he clear defined
And through his laws the hoards of Mortmain land declined
Which corporate bodies and the clergy used to get:
The loss of such windfalls they would for long regret!
Then Robert Bruce rallied the Scots to his own flag
And crowned himself at Scone, as proud as Highland stag.
He little knew that he would meet a swift defeat
And to the Irish coast would need to make retreat.
One year would pass before at Loudon Hill he'd rout
The English force when he from hiding ventured out.
Edward in fury rose, these Scots he would subdue,
Even if it should prove the last of things he'd do.
Tempt not the fates, oh mighty king, for death rules all!
When on his way, our king into death's hands would fall,
But even then his stubborn will would not give in.
He ordered his son to fight and fight until he'd win:
'My corpse shall lead the English army at its head.

I will the rebel Scots subdue though I be dead.
Nor bury me until our conquest is complete:
Even in death I'll brook no thought of our defeat!'
Such was the savage temper of that stubborn man.
Few men, alas, do live to realise their plan.
In Edward's reign the justices of the peace were made,
But Jews were cruelly treated and oft banned from their
  trade.
A sorry plight! A curse of God seems on their race,
What chronicles of suffering must these people face!
Yet Edward was a loving man, who, where his queen
Eleanor's corpse from Grantham to London stopped between,
Stone crosses he had raised to mark each tragic spot,
That her last journey's rests should never be forgot.
Much of our royal Windsor Castle too he built:
Let us think well of those now dead; forgive their guilt.
The bad they did is dead, their good shall e'er prevail,
For light and darkness forms the substance of man's tale.


## Edward II

Edward II weak in mind soon proved to be.
With worthless men, alas, he kept wrong company.
Piers Gaveston, his favourite, he even made
His regent when he sailed to wed a royal maid,
Sweet Isabella, daughter of France's king.
This was a careless, unwise and foolish thing,
For Gaveston became overbearing in extreme
When he more power had beyond his wildest dream.
The angry nobles rose and seized this hapless fool,
Cut off his head to show they despised his rule.
So badly did the king mismanage this fair realm,

28

The nobles by ordinances at last took o'er the helm.
His new oppressive tax they repealed with all due speed,
Binding the king to what their parliament decreed,
Which once a year, or more, henceforth would sit in state
And by its watchful will determine England's fate.
Meanwhile in Scotland Robert Bruce with each attack
Most of the fortresses with martial skill won back.
Almost alone stood Stirling Castle's frowning might;
Public unrest in England meant Edward had to fight.
One hundred thousand men at arms marched out to war
Against the thirty thousand men of Bruce before
The field at Bannockburn. Oh fateful, tragic day
In which the portents speak: listen to what they say!
An English knight, greedy for glory's lasting fame,
With levelled lance at Bruce full galloping he came.
All held their breath and watched in silent awe to see
To whom the fates allow the victor proud to be.
Bruce, waiting quietly, watched his foe draw nigh,
Then swerved and struck the head as he went headlong by.
Before the Scottish horde that knight all lifeless fell:
Loud from the ranks there rose the baying victor's yell.
Nor fared the English horse a better fate than this:
Upon a thousand hidden stakes they plunge and twist
(The ground was dug with pits and pointed stakes were hid
By cunning clumps of earth that formed an artful lid.)
Then Robert Bruce, the brave, led out the charge in line:
'Kill, kill the king, then Scotland's throne shall be all mine!'
Edward fled fast before the foe to Dunbar's shore,
Embarked at once for England, to return no more.
Scotland the brave at last her independence secured,
Flung off the English yoke that she so long endured.
Foul plague and famine ravaged England's countryside:
Weak men attract disasters from every side.

Like many men who find that they're too weak to rule,
Edward sought out his favourites to play the fool.
The angry nobles now exiled the Spencer clique,
To which the king, unlike his wont, reacted quick.
Defeats nobles at Boroughbridge, Lancaster kills,
Imprisoned Mortimer, which added to royal ills,
For he escaped to France to meet the English queen,
To beg of her, for England's sake, to intervene.
Assembles she a force, invades this sorry land,
To free us from her husband's favourites she planned
And so protect her son from Edward's inept reign.
The king fled to the west; the Spencers were caught again:
This time the hangman's noose made sure of their demise;
A favourite has no friend, there's hate in others' eyes.
Edward, compelled by force, resigned his royal crown
And to his son, fourteen, it was now handed down.
Then, when a rising might release the former king,
Cold Mortimer decided he'd not allow such thing:
The former king in secret by a burning rod
Was killed most hideously. Have mercy, God!
Thus ends a life too weak to wield the sword of state.
He was his own worst foe: he caused his own sad fate!
With the Venetian empire England wisely made
A treaty governing the normal terms of trade,
And introduced those bills of 'change which soon would lead
The commercial heart of London Town to richly breed.
Alas, the Knights Templars were in this reign suppressed,
A noble band of men by all it was confessed.
On feeble Edward closed for good sad history's play,
And let us hope and pray there dawns a brighter day!
Queen Isabella with her favourites held power
O'er hapless England at this dire disgraceful hour.
The council of the regent could but idly talk

When they in Mortimer's unscrupulous shadow walk.
Even the Scots invade this land to win their prize
Of independence true before the whole world's eyes.
As long as might is exercised, men firmly hold
Whate'er they want – fair lands, good lives, fine gems and
   gold –
But let them weakness show, and all they won is lost,
Nor be gained back except at great, most hideous cost,
Whilst he whose rule is based upon a borrowed fame
Is bound to fall at last in ignomy and shame.
Thus Mortimer was seized by the maturing king
And Isabella too a captive 'neath his wing,
For life imprisonment for her was all that's left
While murd'rous Mortimer was put at once to death.
And English noblemen soon rush to draw the sword
Until their rich estates in Scotland were restored,
For Robert Bruce's death by then was widely known,
And he succeeded by his son David alone.
Edward supports instead Scottish Balliol's claim:
As Robert Bruce's grandson he was bred for fame
And Scotland's crown would be his own with England's aid.
When David fled to France, our king his regent slayed
In the hard, bitter battle of Halidon Hill
O'er which e'en now the mourning winds blow cold and
   chill.
Next Edward wages war upon the king of France,
Whose throne he claimed was his and bravely seeks his
   chance.
But France abetting Scotland was the reason for
This warrior king to chance his arms in foreign war.
He claimed the throne of France through his own
   mother's line:
Females could not then reign, but gave her son so fine

31

A gift of royal throne. 'Twas not the queen's to give,
But 'what is right' is seldom how men choose to live.
The mighty ever seek to bend the rules of law,
Nor scruple to remake what it was not before.
Conveying troops across the Channel's narrow strait,
He adds to his weak claim his mobile army's weight
And soundly wins off Sluys a famous naval fight
Putting the Genoese and French warships to flight.
Unchecked, our army ravaged the land of Normandy,
Advances up to the very gate of fair Paris,
From out of which the French, a hundred thousand strong,
Descend in rage upon the daring English throng.
'Tis best to bide one's time than face direct defeat,
Edward, though fast pursued, now beat a quick retreat
Until he reached the Somme, a river whose name is dire,
Upon whose flanks the cream of youth in wars expire.
Though Edward forged a passage to the other shore,
He looked dismayed upon the open plains before:
Retreat through open fields would be a fatal plan.
Thus fate now intervened: he must here make his stand.
By Crécy drew he up his men in battle line,
No sun upon his armoured men came out to shine,
But stormy rain and lightning with thunder's boom,
Like awful omens came at dawn, predicting doom.
Then drenching rain like tears came flooding from the sky,
As if heartbroken for the brave about to die.
But stoically, the English stood their sodden ground
Until at noon the midday bell did loudly sound.
When through the easing rain they saw the French advance,
Though drenched right through they chose to take their
      fatal chance.
The Genoese bowmen's exposed bow-strings hung loose,
Their singing arrows fell too short, and were no use,

Whilst English archers unpacked their still-dry bows,
Unleashed their deadly hail upon their deadly foes.
Before this lethal rain the Genoese retreat,
Only to be cut down when charging French they meet.
Here fell blind King John, Bohemian king,
Of whose blind courage let us pause to sing:
To mount a steed and join the battle's angry roar
For sighted man is brave; for blind, how much, much more.
Alas, he fell, but his three-ostrich-feathered crest
With words 'Ich Dien' ('I serve') our Black Prince possessed
And ever since by Prince of Wales so proudly borne,
All honour to that brave blind king whom none dare scorn.
This way and that the line of battle reeled and swayed
As callous fate with fickle dice of warfare played.
From hilltop's height, proud Henry saw his son at war:
Although at times the fiery foe did press him sore,
The king refused to send aid: "Twould be amiss,
Oh, let him win his spurs and let the day be his!'
An anxious father trusts the son he's brought up well,
Though he in peril be within the jaws of hell.
The Black Prince, just sixteen years of age, well fought
And lasting fame and glory on his name was brought.
Two months elapsed and Scotland's king our realm invades,
The Border once again resounds to clashing blades.
But all in vain. This ally of the French reaped loss,
King David was caught, made prisoner at Neville's Cross
By Philippa, our sovereign queen so brave and fair:
A she-wolf guards her home when her fierce mate's not
    there.
In France proud Calais fell to Edward's year-long siege
And to the English throne betrothed her tardy liege.
The English king insists the burgher chiefs must die,
To teach the foolish French the price when they defy.

But Philippa restrained the royal hand from vengeful deed
And all the hapless burghers from their chains were freed.
The power men possess grows ever more sublime
When they show mercy at victory's sweet time.
Alas, with war renewed, the Black Prince rode through France:
See how his warriors boast! See how his chargers prance!
The taste of glorious victory was in the very air:
They captured John, the king of France, defeated at Poitiers.
At Bretigny a solemn treaty then was signed:
All Aquitaine, Guienne and Calais were to us assigned,
Whilst in return Edward forever would renounce
(Only in victory the truth will men announce)
His dubious claim to make the throne of France his own.
A ransom of three million crowns was also thrown
On King John's head – much too high for France to raise,
So John returned, by honour bound, much to his praise,
Into his captor's clutches until the day he died,
At Savoy Palace in the Strand, where he'd reside!
A noble king, too proud to choose the coward's way
Which seeks by fleeing far to win another day.
All wise men know that what we do makes what we are,
And from this self we cannot flee, go we so far
Unto the very ends of this untrodden world,
For in our hearts, what we become lies always curled.
One son the Black Prince sired, a future king,
But for himself no coronation bells would ring.
In one fierce fight the Black Prince won to great renown,
When Pedro of Castile was from his throne cast down.
He won the battle of Navarette, but hollow was that win,
When faithless allies would never pay back to him
The dire expenses of the war, met from his own wealth.
Our prince turned home, in debt and shattered in his health,
To die nine years on, just twelve months before the king,

Who had become an idle, careless and useless thing,
Losing all French possessions except for fair Calais –
And yet he had been most ambitious in his day.
He bit off more than he could chew and had to plead
With parliament for cash supplies to fuel his need.
The payer called the tune and privileges demanded:
Ah, thus the great commander found himself commanded.
And yet throughout his reign the law was well applied,
Prosperity his people knew on every side.
Against the king upon his high and lonely throne
The fierce, ambitious men, like dogs which fight for bone,
Prowl round with snarling, drooling jaws and hungry eyes.
Uneasy rests the head a weary king down lies.
Fine Flemish weavers were encouraged to settle here,
Which would assist commerce the English e'er held dear.
The Lords and Commons too began to sit apart:
From little seeds like this oak trees do make their start.
Swift from the steppes of Asia swept the plague 'Black Death':
At least one third of Europe ceased to draw life's breath.
In the wasteful wake of this most dreadful bane,
The quarrels of the French and English kings aside were lain.
When nature slays with wanton rage, what need man's spite:
Beneath the shadow of its force, man cowers in fright!


**Richard II**

'The king is dead. Long live the king!' Though but a boy,
Richard II was hailed with great, expectant joy,
For much too much was anticipated of one
Who bore the title of the Black Prince's son!
At first that splendid promise seemed to be fulfilled,
Then Wat Tyler's Kentish men, by much anger steeled,

Against an unfair poll tax waged a civil war
And suddenly raised a hoarse, rebellious roar.
En masse they march on London with fast-growing hordes
To face the king and mounted knights with unsheathed
  swords.
They fought at Smithfield and Wat Tyler there was slain,
For insolence he showed to his young king's good name.
The incensed mob sought vengeance for their leader's death,
Until Richard, sixteen years old, with lion's breath,
And fearlessly among them rode and cried,
'Angry and sad are ye that your own man has died.
I am your king and will your future leader be:
Come, rally to my side and follow, follow me!'
O'erawed, they followed him into the open fields
Where he to some of their demands reluctant yields.
But these soon after were revoked, mob leaders slain:
So much revolt, so much anger, so little gain.
How oft a well-begun becomes a feeble end.
Richard's fair promise to his government descends.
At first his ministers by lords appellant bold
Were overthrown and parliament itself annulled.
Next year the king took charge and ruled both wise and
  well:
Who could his future plans in these eight years foretell?
For now Richard took a firm, despotic rule,
Only one year beyond that parliament called 'wonderful'.
The lords appellant he had killed or banished far
And forced his parliament to rob our money jar,
To make his rule thus independent of them all.
As ever, pride and greed precede close on a fall.
He quarrelled badly with his cousin Bolingbroke:
A mind intent on ill can soon disputes provoke.
He quarrelled with the Dukes of Lancaster and Norfolk too,

A course of confrontation which one day he'd rue.
He banished Bolingbroke for ten long weary years
And adds another insult to his kinsfolk's tears,
For whilst away his father John of Gaunt has died,
Without his son to keep a vigil by his side.
Harsh Richard seized unjustly John of Gaunt's estates:
Such arrogance at once attracts the wrathful fates.
The king in Ireland avenges the Earl of March's death
And many families there were of their sons bereft.
Duke Bolingbroke at Ravenspur in Yorkshire lands,
Recruits the discontented nobles to his bands,
Including Percys and the Nevilles, whose great fame
Our island's future historians would oft proclaim.
When sixty thousand men bore arms against the king,
Poor Richard found his royal cause a hopeless thing.
At Conway he was seized, his crown he must resign
And defeated died, the last of Plantagenet's line.
Some say that in Pontefract's high castellated keep
He starved to death or was slain, perhaps in sleep.
Yet others hoped he'd escaped to Scotland's waste,
To die when very old, in no unseemly haste.


## Henry IV

It matters not – 'The king is dead, long live the king!' –
For Henry IV usurps the throne he claims as king.
So ends this unifying Plantagenet age
In which so many, many bitter battles rage.
But all is not a tale of unrelenting gloom,
For oft from dire events which seem to spell dark doom
There comes some good when men react against great wrong,
As when they rose against the tyranny of John,

Normans and Saxons joined into one nation free,
Forcing King John to sign the Magna Carta decree.
Thus former bitter foes will often firm unite
When jointly they a common greater evil fight.
So, as the Plantagenet kings' thirst grew for war,
On parliament for funds they need rely far more.
But he who pays the piper always calls the tune,
Gaining more privileges and sway, 'til all too soon
The power absolute of kings becomes curtailed.
For he who borrows free soon by his debts is jailed
And binds himself and all he has unto the will
Of those most keen his hungry pockets deep to fill.
When England's lords rode out to fight Crusades abroad:
They opened up the East, and trade followed the sword,
And from the East (a mixed blessing would come of this)
Brought back fine paper which the scribes would find
    sweet bliss.
Yes! From the East fine paper was transported back,
That indispensable stuff of which there's now no lack!
A boon often becomes a burden by excess:
In years to come a flood of paper spewed from each press,
A bureaucratic tide engulfed each governed state,
Nor does it seem this paper surge will e'er abate!
The middle class grew very rich and could afford
To buy the sore neglected homes of absent lord,
While Flemings settled here when Henry III was king,
And taught the art of woollen manufacturing.
Which in the years to come great wealth to us provides,
Emboldened English merchant ships to brave the tides.
Within their high-walled towns the merchants dwelt at ease,
Windows of glass and chimneys tall their wives would please.
Mariner's compass steered their ships through oceans far,
More certain than the light of cloud-enveloped star.

Their growing wealth created another source of work
For those who from the nobles' feudal rule would shirk.
It formed a useful check against the barons' might,
Who feudal dominance believed was theirs by right.
At York, Winchester and Salisbury cathedrals rise:
Their Gothic decorated styles now grace our skies.
While Chaucer, founding father of English poetry,
Recorded his joyous lines for all posterity.
His *Canterbury Tales* encapsulate the age –
The good, the bad, the wit, the scold, the fool and sage –
The poor man's poet, Langland, *Piers Plowman* wrote.
From both, stern tutors love to long, obscurely quote!
Meanwhile John Wycliffe, father first of English prose,
Laid well the base from which our lovely language rose.
Lancastrian Henry IV usurps the throne
And claimed this noble realm as his and his alone.
The rightful heir, Edmund, kept in mild captivity,
Was like a cagéd bird, well kept but never free.
The English crown was elective and is still,
And Henry was the popular choice of natural will –
But doubtful deeds long shadows cast, and future years
In civil war would reap the price in futile tears.
Weigh well the consequences of what you choose to do,
Lest you or distant heirs your hasty action rue.
The lowland Scots, by Douglas led, invade our land,
But they reckoned without the Earl of Northumberland.
Illlustrious Percy served his king and country well,
Made Douglas prisoner as many Scotsmen fell.
But Henry caused offence by forbidding him to claim
A ransom for their prisoner's great Scottish fame.
For Henry hoped more gainful terms himself to make,
Although with loyal friends this could only cause a break.
The Percys then allied themselves with Scottish clans

And joined with Glendower's Welsh warrior bands.
Henry defeated the Percys before they could unite,
At Shrewsbury's battlefield in one great show of might.
Henry Hotspur, alas, at battle's height was slain,
Short-lived, his father's loss and inconsolable pain.
For he soon faced defeat: Northumberland was killed,
At Bramham Moor beside a sad, despondent field.
The Lollards, by Wycliffe led, had reforming zeal,
Were harassed by the king to gain the church's goodwill –
A ruse oft-times adopted by those who choose to rule:
Indifferent to right, they let expediency pull.
The Scottish prince, who would King James I become,
Was captured as he fled to France, but stayed not dumb.
He whiled away imprisonment in Windsor's keep
By writing there a lovely poem of feelings deep
In honour of his lady love, sweet Lady Joan,
Who on release he made as queen his very own.
Though prison chains may bind the body's listless clay,
Yet none can e'er the restless, soaring spirit stay.
At forty-six King Henry met his early death,
Nor all his strength could stay that last escaping breath.
For fourteen years King Henry o'er England had reigned,
In which our parliament more privileges gained
With freedom of debate, that precious, priceless gem,
From which much good in future would most surely stem.
The Order of the Bath was by the king bestowed,
Whose members had to bathe, a sign of loyalty owed,
For they were deemed as pure in body as in mind.
A ritual such as this would more securely bind
Than could the chains of bronze or granite fortress walls:
Before the flattery of pomp even the greatest falls.

# Henry V

Henry V renewed a ruthless war with France –
An insult from the Dauphin affords the chance –
And he revived his ancient long outstanding claim
To add the envied throne of France to his domain.
His real intent: to dazzle minds with martial glory,
Distract the mob by far-off battlefields so gory.
Thereby a civil war he cunningly averts:
Usurper's son, all too aware of his just deserts!
And thus the seething discontent of rightful heirs
Diverts by foreign war all thoughts of what is theirs,
For what in peace is just a claim with right and reason
In war, by undermining state, becomes foul treason!
Henry beseiged Harfleur, and then at Agincourt
A hard and decisive battle he fiercely fought –
With sharply pointed stakes driven into the ground,
Which all the English forward ranks on foot surround
To hide them from the French cavalry's wild charge,
Impaling many of the horse, however large,
While on the dense, confuséd masses the archers rain,
From stout longbows, volleys of deadly stinging pain.
Then, then the English charged againt the French melee,
Killing with ease or taking captive e'er they could flee.
All down the ages men the stout longbow would praise
That won for England's king this best of all great days.
But all too soon the war with France was joined anew:
The Duke of Burgundy, in Dauphin's sight, they slew,
Which caused his son in fear to join the English force.
Fair France was thus divided by this dire divorce,
Until at Troyes a treaty true was firmly sealed
By which, to Henry, France her Catherine would yield –
A princess proudly won by force of superior might

Which could in time the throne of France with ours unite,
For as the regent now of France, Henry could claim
The right of succession in his illustrious name.
Alas, the dreams of men like dust so quickly fly,
For at the height of their success they die.
Thus died this valiant king at only thirty-five;
His doubtful claim to rule was won by dashing drive.
No one condemns a ruling king who still succeeds:
The mob is quick beguiled by daring, winning deeds.
The national navy, by King Alfred first begun,
Was built by Henry into an independent one,
Henceforth no longer on our merchant ships relying
Whose greed, delays and means proved often deeply trying.
In this king's reign London was first with lanterns lit,
The leader of the Lollards torched to add to it –
A heretic no doubt to those of older views,
But how such acts gainsay what's preached in holy pews!
Oft man purports to praise his God of love in church
When in his heart of hearts for love we vainly search.
Instead of making this sad earth a better place,
By evil acts in God's name we bring yet more disgrace.


## Henry VI

Henry VI was but a child when he succeeded,
So counsels of older, wiser men were needed.
His uncle, Gloucester's duke, was chosen to take charge,
Was made 'Protector', these royal duties to discharge.
Another uncle, John the duke of Bedford, was installed
As regent of fair France which England still o'er-ruled.
Although the Dauphin, Charles, disputed this valid claim,
Forgetting 'bout the treaty made at Troyes, whose fame

Could not be easily forgot at princely whim:
This foolish claim brought down the English wrath on him.
A notable victory by Bedford o'er France was won:
At Rouvrai were once more the valiant French o'ercome.
They launched a new attack upon the luckless English
As they were fetching vital supplies of fresh salt-fish
('The Battle of the Herring', as it was soon known),
The unsustainability of our attack was shown
When we our lengthened supply lines could not defend,
Nor on a hostile populace for food depend.
The seige of Orleans proved the final watershed
Which to the loss of power by the English led.
Their troubles were hastened on by Bedford's death,
Compounded when the Duke of Burgundy soon left.
Our English side, rejoining now the French again,
Saw fortress after fortress by French forces regain,
Until only Calais remained in English hands.
Some good would come from loss of these near lands:
In future times without the continental realm
The English many distant countries would overwhelm.
Warwick and Earl Edward returned to defeat the king
And into prison harsh this hapless man did fling.
A peasant maiden, Joan of Arc, from the Lorraine,
Revived the failing fortunes of fair France again.
Sad sights of suffering, destruction and the dead,
Such horrors of war filled her heart with dread.
She felt profound pity for her homelands of France:
Uncannily strong, she became like one in trance.
Her heart was filled with an absorbing passion
That she, as prophecies foretold, through God would fashion
A fresh resolve for France, to save that lovely land
And cause the once-defeated turn and make a stand.
Not through her choice, but by the Lord's almighty will,

Nor could her parents, priest or soldiers stop or still
The burning flame that set her mind and heart on fire
With one fantastic, patriotic, firm desire.
There is no power on this earth that can restrain
A single-minded will that once ignites the brain.
The human spirit, once aroused, and come what may,
Will ever overcome the worst and have its way.
So to the Dauphin came this slight and lowly maid
And told him of her mission straight and unafraid:
That he would be anointed and crowned in Rheims,
Become lieutenant of God, as was told in her dreams.
Then, clothed in armour white from haughty head to toe,
Upon a charger white she rode to meet the foe.
From victory to victory her armies led,
And left the hated English wounded, shamed or dead.
She raised the seige of fair Orleans and on to Rheims,
Fulfilled her holy mission and realised her dreams.
With Dauphin crowned as king, no further vows to keep,
She begged that she return to home to tend her sheep.
The king detained the maid to serve her country more –
A royal command she would soon enough deplore.
Imprisoned, the maid to Burgundy was sold,
Who gave her to the English for his Judas gold.
She was treated as a witch with great brutality,
And suffered much in spite of meekness and purity.
No soldier fierce would dare admit defeat by her,
Lest he the mockery of others would incur.
Such strength in one so frail to sorcery was due:
How else could a mighty force be beaten by so few?
At Rouens market square they burnt her at the stake,
But never once did she her faith in God forsake.
'My voices were of God,' she bravely cried aloud
As searing flames surrounded her like a blazing shroud.

And just before she was engulfed by greedy flames,
A cry of 'Jesus!' she defiantly proclaims.
One English soldier in soulful shame hung his head:
'We are now lost, we've burnt a saint,' he softly said.
As Henry, quiet and harmless, grew to be a man,
He proved unfit to govern well our rich and noble land.
So he was wed to Margaret, princess of fair Anjou,
A strong-minded woman who could rule as well as two.
Princess of Provence proud, she soon assumed full power
And before her strong resolve her husband could but cower.
'The keys of Normandy', Anjou and Maine, were given up
Through Duke of Suffolk's guile: and when strong protests
    erupt,
And at the king's behest, he tried to flee to France
But fate intervened to hinder his hapless chance.
His flight was blocked at sea and he was beheaded there,
Alone with none alongside his shameful guilt to share.
Beneath a feeble king the barons for control vie:
Under a battlefield this country long did lie
As they put their own gain above the nation's good,
Which common folk have never fully understood,
For on their backs the burden falls most hard.
Would that a lasting peace such civil wars retard!
Led by Jack Cade, the vengeful peasants made revolt,
Commit outrages, took London as their last insult,
Until with promises of pardon they disband,
Returning home once more to labour on the land.
But Cade was slain in combat in a Kentish garden:
For leaders of revolt there can never be a pardon.
Harsh rulers know the real ringleaders must be caught –
How else the lessons of acceptance be well taught?
Unmask just once the face of false authority,
And none shall bow again to sham superiority!

For Cade's revolt was just a sign of what people thought
About Duke Richard, who the throne of England sought.
Lancastrians and Yorkists both claimed the royal throne,
Each took up arms to seize it for their very own.
Richard, the Duke of York, adopts a pure white rose;
Lancastrians under Prince John of Gaunt oppose
And bore a blood-red rose as their proud badge of war.
Richard of York, against a childless king, once swore
That he him would succeed, become a ruling king,
But fate would act to thwart the chance of such a thing.
A son and heir to Henry now at last was born
And Richard's fond ambitious hopes became forlorn.
The daring claims of Richard sent the king insane:
As his protector, Richard vied the crown to gain,
But soon the king recovered full his feeble wits,
Releasing Somerset in one of his much saner fits.
In anger Yorkists rose in arms against the crown,
Defeated the Duke of Somerset and cut him down.
The king was captured by the duke and went insane,
So Richard thus became Protector once again.
The feeble king recovered, had the duke dismissed,
But the Yorkists, angered by this unexpected twist,
Resumed the War of the Roses with renewed vim,
Attacked Lord Dudley at Bloreheath, defeated him,
They joined the daring Duke of York at Ludlow, where
Henry VI with sixty thousand men repair.
On sight of these the Yorkists fled in great alarm,
Far better flee to France or Ireland than face harm.
Then Warwick with King Edward's help defeats the king
And into prison foul their royal prize they fling.
Brazenly then the Duke of York the throne loud claims,
Hoping to achieve at last his high, ambitious aims.
While weakly Henry wears, by compromise, the crown

While he still lives, but on his death it would pass down,
Not to his son and heir, but to Duke Richard, who
By ancient right of conquest claimed it as his due.
They reckoned ill who left the fearless, brave queen out:
She with her son escaped to Scotland, soon to rout
And stop proud Richard when returning with great force,
Displayed his head at York (with paper crown of course)
To underline the folly of his futile aims
And as a lesson to all who might make false claims.
Lord Salisbury was next to feel the axe's steel:
The final way to finish foes is them to kill.
Then Margaret advanced on London Town to wage
Her war on Warwick, who was forced to ope' the cage.
Reluctantly he let the weak, imprisoned king go free:
None a more eventful life had any king than he!
Before Edward the Duke of York could march to aid,
The Warwick forces now great resistance displayed.
Compelling Margaret's mighy army to retreat,
His popularity soon led to her defeat.
For with the help of Warwick, Edward proclaimed
As king and Warwick 'The Kingmaker' was thereafter named.
Yet Henry's reign had seen the start of statute law
In place of petitions, as was the case before:
All statutory bills had first to gain assent
Of both kings and lords; all law was by their consent.


## Edward IV

Edward IV from Warwick and the Neville clan
Received support, but Margaret's fierce warrior band
Still held on to the north, where proud Warwick sped
And fought a battle dire from which his forces fled.

If he could not recall his troops, he'd face defeat:
He had to stop his army's rapid, headlong retreat.
Dismounting from his trusty steed, his sword he drew
And swiftly ran a poor unfortunate soldier through.
With all escape confounded, he had no choice but try
To meet the foe on foot and not afraid to die
Upon the battlefield, though all his men depart:
On sight of him, they rallied round to take his part.
Defeating Duke of Somerset in bloody fight;
King Henry and his queen to Scotland made their flight,
Then later to the continent with haste they fled,
Soon at Hexham the Duke of Somerset lay dead.
Alas, King Henry was to his enemies foul betrayed
And to the Tower of London was swiftly conveyed.
Kingmaker Warwick, by Edward IV offended,
Chose to wreak revenge: that careless reign he ended.
Releasing Henry from his cheerless prison cell,
He gravely gave him back his royal throne as well.
King Edward fled to Holland, vowing to return
And fight against the man who dared his rule to spurn.
With Charles the Bold of Burgundy's resourceful aid,
A massive landing on the Yorkshire coast was made,
Where Yorkists flocked en masse to join his banner bold –
A wondrous sight which all en route in awe behold.
At Barnet's Field a decisive combat was fought,
Where victorious Edward the fleeing Warwick caught.
And with his brother Montague was put to death,
Only Queen Margaret at Tewkesbury was left.
Where Lancastrians their long last battle lost,
And hapless Henry back into the Tower tossed.
Proud Margaret's Edward was by his uncles killed,
Then Henry's execution by Edward was willed.
In 1473 the king laid claim to France,

Invaded in force to press with strength his chance.
But soon a truce for seven years by treaty made,
Provided an annuity by France was paid.
He next his brother Clarence held for treason high,
Who in a butt of Malmsey wine did drowning die.
The king himself in 1493 was dead
And Edward his son at eleven would reign instead.
Within the late king's reign, Caxton set up his press:
Who could foretell how great would be its long success?
No more would scribe with quill and ink on vellum write
A single copy, striving hard to get it right!
While post, from London Town to Scotland, by high road
Was sped on flying horse as fast as spurs could goad.
Edward extracted forced loans from the poor folk,
The first to suffer from his harsh, unyielding yoke.
Two rival kings claimed simultaneously the state,
Whilst Warwick broods which one of them to reinstate.
The eldest son Edward eleven weeks would reign:
When he to London Town travelled with royal train,
Via Stoney Stratford, that he might be crowned as king
And hear the oaths of sworn allegiance his nobles bring,
His enemies conspired to stop this solemn deed
And Richard, Duke of Gloucester, on his zealous steed
Attacked the royal band, arrested the would-be king
And, with his brother, into the bloody Tower did fling.
'All this I do for their own safety,' he said,
As poisonous tales about the former king he spread.
He took the title of 'Protector', killing those
Who might his vaunting high ambitious aims oppose.

# Richard III

Then, with the aid of Buckingham, he took the throne,
To rule as king himself and all its powers own.
Uneasy rests the crafty head that steals a crown,
Suspecting others who all unsmiling gather round.
Unwise, he thought, to let his 'protected' nephews live,
Who to other schemers in time excuse could give,
Seeking to reinstate the lawful king instead,
Snatching the stolen crown from the usurper's head.
Imagine the princes asleeping in the Tower,
Awaking suddenly in dreadful fear to cower
As heartless killers raise their cold, unfeeling steel
And these young innocents they ruthlessly kill.
In secret is this shameful deed undertaken,
But guilt is never by false alibis e'er shaken.
The finger points to him who stands to gain the most
And future trends are shaped by shadows of their ghost.
Richard Crookshank had cause enough to fear his 'friends':
Ambition seen to succeed tempts all to try such ends.
E'en Buckingham, the chief supporter of the king,
Conspired the Earl of Richmond to the throne to bring.
Betrayed by Bannister, Buckingham was caught
And was beheaded for his schemes which came to naught.
The way we act is copied by those in the know,
And we unwitting reap the evil which we sow.
This law applies alike to rulers and the ruled,
None may escape: the way of nature can't be fooled.
When Richard landed in force at Milford Haven in Wales,
He fought a fearful battle at Bosworth Field, but fails:
Although he fought most bravely, he at length was slain,
So ended Richard Crookshank's brief and troubled reign.

## Henry VII

After the battle in a bush the crown was found
And on the head of Earl of Richmond was placed around.
Thus Henry Tudor now ascended the English throne,
A title which he could not claim, in truth, as his own.
To strengthen his fragile position he'd propose
To wed Elizabeth, known as England's white rose –
The daughter of Edward IV, which reconciled
The Yorkists and Lancastrians from feuding wild.
The rightful heir into the Tower he next threw,
Which caused the insurrections that he would soon rue.
In Ireland insurrection through one Simnel came,
Who as Earl of Warwick made outrageous claim.
A priest from Oxford called Simon supports his role,
And Simnel soon in England lands to pursue his goal.
But by De Vere, Simnel was dealt a grave defeat:
His leader Earl of Lincoln slain, Simnel was beat,
Contemptly made a scullion in the kitchen's soil,
In heat and steam and waste with endless menial toil
To live a drudge's life, until he would make good,
Become a falconer to hunt the royal wood.
But still some folk believed that he was Warwick's earl,
Despite the king displaying Warwick to dispel
Their false belief, though once a rumour is well told,
Upon the public it acquires a steadfast hold.
Next insurrection by a Perkin Warbeck came,
Who said Richard Duke of York was his real name,
The brother of Edward V, he claimed, who fled
The bloody Tower when his brother was found dead.
He was assisted by James IV, the Scottish king,
Who gave in marriage Lady Gordon to bind with ring
His protégé, lest he his Scottish help disown

Should he successfully ascend the English throne.
The sister of Edward IV also backed him,
He landed on the Cornish beaches full of vim.
Alas, his lofty regal aims were swift reversed
His band of Irish followers were fast dispersed.
So in the Tower ended ambition's short reign:
So much futile effort for but so little gain.
Within the Tower Perkin made a dangerous friend,
For on the Earl of Warwick he came to depend.
The hapless two attempted their escape to make,
But in this enterprise the fates would both forsake.
And so the fate-forsaken two were put to death
And of their unwise conspiracy nothing was left.
The knight who saved King Henry's life on Bosworth Field,
And handed him the crown, found that a feeble shield –
For William Stanley was put to death as well,
But was it for his wealth, or treason? Who could tell?
The tallest ears of corn attract the scyther's blade
And wealth, amassed in life, by death is soon unmade.
King Henry, by the marriage of his eldest son
To Spanish princess Catherine of Aragon,
His influence and power sought further to extend:
Oh, what will man not do to reach his chosen end?
Treating his children like pawns in his great game,
Without compassion nor an ounce of shame.
Alas, within six months Prince Arthur sadly died.
Unwilling to repay the dowry for the bride,
King Henry gave his second eldest son instead
The early-widowed grieving wife at once to wed.
His daughter Margaret he married to King James
Of Scotland, bringing both realms within his claims.
He married his youngest daughter to Louis of France.
Is there nothing an ambitious man won't chance?

And afterwards to Brandon, Duke of Suffolk, wed,
Which union finally to Lady Jane Grey led.
King Henry sent to Ireland Sir Poyning, whose law
Made English rule hold sway in Ireland, so before
Any Irish parliament could sit, the king's consent
Had first to be obtained, a rule we'd long relent.
In future years this would only cause great conflict,
You cannot others with impunity restrict.
King Henry's character was one of purest greed:
He levied from his subjects too much to fund his need
To wage a war on France, discontinuing it when
King Charles offered to him a great fortune to spend.
But hoard, not spend, was his design: his palace at Sheen
Was filled with the greatest fortune ever seen.
Of what import is wealth when each life ends in death?
For when we die no fortune buys just one more breath.
In 1509 King Henry died at fifty-two:
So closed the Middle Ages; its feudal system too.
The art of printing was rediscovered again,
For waking man a cultural, long-abiding gain.
As barbarism by classic learning was dispelled,
There seemed to be the dawn of a new and better
    world.
Columbus sailed exploring the New World's wild coast,
While Cabot could Newfoundland's discovery boast,
And Vasco da Gama sailed round the Cape to blaze
A path to India's wealth which all the world would
    praise.
At home the court of the Star Chamber was revived
Which punished state affairs, the slower laws o'errided.
With Burgundy was forged a good commercial deal
Whose benefits for continental trade were real.
King Henry further fostered England's naval sway,

A legacy that helped this realm unto this modern day.
He built a mighty man-of-war, *Great Harry* called,
With which the Channel Straits were safely ruled.


## Henry VIII

At eighteen years of age Henry VIII became the king
And gave his brother's widow his own wedding ring.
By executing Empson, then Dudley, who tax extorted
For his late brother's many wars, he quickly courted
The popularity of his trusty subjects:
All praise to him who past injustice firm rejects!
When war broke out with France, he won the Battle of
   Spurs,
So called because the French retreated like frightened curs,
Using their spurs much more than swords against their foes.
With Henry away at war, King James of Scotland chose
To march on England and invade its defenceless land,
But by this rash decisive act he betrayed his hand.
At Flodden Field Scots met defeat and King James was slain:
This left on Scottish history a gory stain –
The flower of the Scottish nobles most cruelly killed,
And all the nation's aspirations and wild hopes were stilled.
Queen Margaret, as regent for her infant son,
Sued for a peace which she from brother Henry won.
Soon the unwise war with France came to a timely end
The two young kings, Henry and Francis, now extend
Their hands in friendship, planned a tournament to be held
In which all pageantry in plumes and flags proud furled,
So brilliantly dressed a sight all would behold,
Forever more was called 'the Field of Cloth of Gold'.
Long days and nights the French and English nobles fêted,

Such gallant merriment their youthful spirits created,
Until homeward they turned with hearts refreshed with joy,
Though such extravagance some wiser heads annoy.
But none can take away such rich and lasting mem'ries,
For life is made of such momentous days as these.
Here Cardinal Wolsey, Henry's wise chancellor,
Ably and fairly administered England's law.
From humble birth he rose too fast to giddy heights
And many noble men suffered his stinging slights.
He treated them with scorn as greater power came
And thought himself the sole creator of his fame.
He built a splendid household that rivalled the king's;
Proud knights and barons dined amidst luxurious things.
At Hampton Court and Whitehall stood his lovely homes
And in his enormous library were rich and costly tomes.
Favoured by the Pope, he was sent a cardinal's hat
As token of his esteem, and made him his legate.
Henry also was made 'Defender of the Faith'
For writing contra Martin Luther and keeping safe
Established religion from extremists' dire reforms,
For nothing pleases those who rule that each conforms –
For those who advocate the virtues of more change
Might well suggest to other men a wider range.
If men query religion, they might question priests,
Then kings and wealthy lords, and challenge their rich feasts.
When Catherine of Aragon her beauty lost,
As illness and advancing years exact harsh cost,
Henry began to doubt how legal 'twas to wed
The wife of his own brother, though he was long dead.
He sought divorce and petitioned the holy Pope,
Who asked Wolsey for his help, raising the king's one hope –
For had he not raised Wolsey up to his high estate?
Alas, the Christian Pope would not his marriage negate,

In spite of pious Wolsey's most persuasive pleas.
A favourite is only such while he can please,
But once he fails his master's whims to realise,
He finds professed friendship but expedient lies.
Enraged, the king dismissed Lord Wolsey from his court:
Another, more compliant chancellor he sought.
He gave the chancellor's great seal to Thomas More
And, not content with this, rubbed salt into the sore:
Wolsey he exiled to York, then called him to the Tower,
But on return Wolsey passed on at death's apt hour.
Before he died, he groaned that had he served his God
The half as he served his king, he would be spared this rod.
The new archbishop, Cranmer, with Henry agreed –
The marriage to Queen Catherine invalid indeed –
As did most university dons when asked their views:
Who could this tyrant king his arguments refuse?
In 1533 fair Anne Boleyn the king did wed,
And Queen Elizabeth I by this union was bred.
Alas, poor Anne was put to death on grounds untrue:
What will a wilful king to get his way not do?
The cruel king soon wed the young Jane Seymour and won
From her the blessing of a longed-for royal son.
Alas, in giving birth frail Seymour lost her life:
Fate robbed the tragic king of his beloved wife.
Next Henry married Anne of Cleves, but when he saw
She was not as charming as portrayed to him before,
And so, she was divorced, freeing the king to wed
Poor Catherine Howard, who all too soon was dead.
She, executed by royal command, thus lost her throne
To Catherine Parr, who survived the tyrant king alone.
Divorce to Catherine Howard had turned most sour
Those once-pious relations with the papal power.
So Henry, after Wolsey's death, boldly proclaim

Himself 'Supreme Head of Church' in fact and name.
Like many who the giddy wine of power taste,
He liked to wield his self-extended power with haste.
His cruel, vindictive and arbitrary rage
Deep casts a dark and dreadful cloud across the age.
Whoever dare oppose the ruthless royal will
Were soon enough beheaded by the axeman's steel.
Two old and faithful servants, Thomas More, his friend,
And Bishop Fisher, both met this ignoble end,
Because they could not Catherine's divorce condone,
Nor hold the king as head of England's church alone.
King Henry feared the monks and friars would undermine
His royal influence and zealous reforming line.
He coveted the wealth the monasteries acquired,
And to achieve the dual ends that he desired
He razed to the ground three thousand monasteries
And stole their wealth, defacing holy effigies –
An act of vandalism that lost for us great art
And tore the nations' holy men of faith apart.
The north of England rose against these royal crimes –
A pilgrimage of grace in these unholy times.
King Henry dispersed them with promises untrue,
Then executed the leaders as he was wont to do.
King Henry was by Cranmer backed, and Cromwell too.
The first he made archbishop; the second, who
Became his vicar general in church affairs,
With zeal added to the monasteries' sad cares.
To please his master, Cromwell went on a looting spree,
But in the king's favours he was not long to be.
The unknown Anne of Cleves he urged the king to wed,
As this would aid the Reformation, so he said.
But Henry liked not Anne and blamed his one-time friend,
Thus came cold Cromwell to a swift and cutting end.

None knew what Henry's religious changes really meant
And each interpreted them according to his bent,
But woe betide the wretched man who got it wrong:
He soon would feel the stinging whip of eightfold thong
(A statute so ambiguously drawn up which may
Both Protestant and Catholic alike soon disobey).
Erring Protestants were burnt at the blazing stake
If they would not the six articles fully take,
While Catholics as traitors to death were likewise led,
Who would not accept King Henry as the church's head.
Even Lord Bishop Latimer, once strong, resigned,
While cautious Thomas Cranmer to Germany his wife
    consigned.
In 1536 Wales was joined to England,
And Henry dubbed himself the king of all Ireland.
Meanwhile for treason Margaret was unjustly slain,
The agéd countess of fair Salisbury Plain.
Who could escape this king's uncertain, wicked whim?
Not those poor souls who were (or seemed) opposed to him!
In 1542 the Scots were soundly beat
At Solway Moss, which broke the heart of James complete.
Hope losing died, to leave young Mary Queen of Scots,
A hapless child unequal to succession plots.
So jealous of the Duke of Norfolk was the king,
And jealous of the son above everything,
He executed the son and would the father too,
But he before evil wicked deed could do,
Himself unloved expired upon that self-same day:
The reaper grim with scythe the king did slay.
Capricious, worldly-wise, irate and fearless too,
Nor state nor church could stop what once he chose to do.
Weak parliaments were slaves unto this king, and let
Not once but twice his heavy debts to quite forget.

They let him settle, too, who should succeed the crown,
For few would dare provoke the tyrant's murd'rous frown.
So he bequeathed it to son Edward and his heirs,
Then next to daughters Mary, Elizabeth: and dares
To set aside the heirs of Margaret, the queen
Of Scotland, who, as elder sister, should have been
Expectant of some recognition of her dues,
But these the wilful tyrant at death's door refuse.
Within this troubled reign ship-building was improved:
The Royal Navy, reorganised, later proved
The saviour more than once of this our tiny isle
When greedy greater nations envied our life's style.
The first of England's ships in 1541
Sailed out to India, and another tale was begun.
Cranmer an English Book of Common Prayer drew,
Which would be preached at church to many, not the few.


## Edward VI

Thus Edward VI at only nine ascended to the throne,
But at this tender age he could never rule alone,
And so his mother's brother, Lord Seymour, became
The Lord Protector, and was king in all but name.
Henry had wished his son to marry the Queen of Scots,
Uniting both these countries, thus he wily plots.
But Mary's countryman would not to this agree,
And Duke Somerset invaded Scotland to press this plea.
So Scots enlist aid from France and sent their queen
To be betrothed to the French Dauphin unseen.
When Somerset became too jealous of his brother
He had him slain, his too-ambitious hopes to smother.
For this unnatural act Duke Somerset was hated,

59

Nor was his arrogance and avarice abated.
He cleared fine churches and bishops' palaces to make land
To build his mansion, Somerset House, by The Strand.
Misgovernment gave cause for insurrections wide,
Both east and west were on rebellion's rising tide:
That in the west due to the state's religious change;
That in the east because enclosures they arrange,
Seizing the common lands and even public parks –
Only the most foolish man upon such theft embarks.
They roused the fury of the Norfolk tanner Ket,
'Til he all Warwick's well-armed men in battle met.
His insurrection crushed by overwhelming might,
Which sadly proves that force will ever vanquish right.
Warwick put Somerset to death, then aiming high,
The throne itself became the focus of his eye.
He caused his son to make Lady Jane Grey his bride,
Induced the dying king to set Mary★ aside
Because she would religion's new reforms oppose –
And shortly thereafter Edward's life came to its close.
Several grammar schools were founded in his reign,
The North-East Passage found brought Russian trading gain.

## Mary

So Henry's daughter Mary became our sovereign queen,
And her future reign of terror was very quickly seen.
But why was Henry's daughter now proclaimed as queen?
The English were on regular succession very keen
And overlooked the fact that like breeds like, but soon
This ill-bred tyrant caused all to dance her tune.

---

★ Edward's sister.

Lady Jane Grey and Lord Dudley were thrown in gaol,
Northumberland was soon beheaded – God rest his soul!
While to the waiting scaffold went the Lady Jane Grey,
Whose death was by insurrections hastened, they say,
Led by Sir Thomas Wyatt to prevent the King of Spain
From taking Mary in marriage, England's realm to gain.
Although Wyatt attacked London, he was soon caught –
And executed: the lesson for treason must be taught.
The queen's own sister, Elizabeth, suspected as well,
Was sent into the Tower, there in fear to dwell.
Brought up as a Catholic, Mary sought to restore
The old Roman faith and papal church once more.
All statutes of King Edward's reign were now repealed
That to the Protestant religious faith appealed.
Imprisoned clergymen were now at once set free,
Returning to their livings, under papal See.
The legate of the Pope was by parliament embraced,
Complete obedience to the papal rules replaced
Protestant faith and rule across fair England's land,
Conspiracies against arose on every hand.
Convicted bishops Hooper, Latimer and Ridley,
And Cranmer were cruelly burnt for heresy,
While Pole, a relative of this reforming queen,
Became archbishop and all was what once had been.
Political agitation then ceased for a while,
Leaving this realm to one fanatical guile.
Mary's husband, Philip II of proud Spain,
Persuaded the queen to war with France yet once again.
The battle of St Quentin saw the French defeated:
For them this dire disgrace the fires of vengeance heated.
Be loath to make attack unless you kill outright,
For in due time your thwarted foe resumes the fight.
The next year, after France recaptured Calais port,

The last of England's land in France. When that report
To Mary was relayed, this national loss she grieved,
Although with foresight she might have been relieved.
'When dead, "Calais" you'll find is written on my heart,'
For Mary held that this French town was of her realm a part.
Our queen not long did grieve this city's tragic loss,
In death's furnace, she was in heated fever, tossed.
Thus fittingly ended her brief but deadly reign:
She who had burnt so many felt death's fiery pain.
To those who revel in conspiracy's sham spells,
The same-day death of kinsman Pole intriguingly tells
Of darker deeds, foul play and timely murder, where
No facts support, except coincidences most rare.
Within her troubled reign the first ambassador
Arrived from Russia's distant dark and icy shore,
Starting a long and lucrative mutual trade:
Firm lines of lasting friendship and commerce thus were laid.
Here colleges of famous Trinity, St John's
Were founded in fair Oxford Town with learned dons,
Whilst on the Roman road fine coaches were introduced,
The rigours of long travel being much reduced.


## Elizabeth I

As after darkness dawns a brighter glorious day,
Whose light becomes the more intense with every ray,
So after Mary's bloody reign the new queen gleamed
And in contrast far more brightly shone on all, it seemed.
Elizabeth undid all that her sister did,
On Catholics' emerging might she closed the lid,
Returned the church to Protestant edicts and rites,
Choosing the great Lord Burleigh for her fights.

Queen Mary of the Scots Elizabeth ill-treated
When the Scots at Pinkie were by her armies defeated.
From thence to France Mary was sent and there she wed
The Dauphin, whose exciting court life went to her head.
When he untimely died, returned to Scotland's shores,
Where her Catholic faith would upset reforming laws.
Many also upset by religious dissent
Which now against the rising Protestantism went.
She married reckless Darnley, husband most unkind,
For too much jealousy unhinged his violent mind.
Before the queen and maids of honour, Rizzio killed,
Her close Italian secretary, whose death he willed.
Poor innocent, sad Rizzio thus untimely died,
But justice, or perhaps revenge, was not denied,
For murd'rous, reckless Darnley was himself blown up:
He who pours in the poison often drains the cup.
Suspicion fell on Mary, though no proof was found,
Then she the powerful Bothwell wed, whose aims unbound
Caused many feckless follower her to desert:
Unwise alliances will only bring one deep hurt.
Her army was defeated at Carberry Hill
She had no choice but bow to her conqueror's will.
She was compelled to pass her crown on to her son
Prince James while she, incarcerated, seemed undone.
But with the aid of Douglas, Mary soon escaped her cell;
Her followers, however, did not fare so well.
They were defeated by the regent Murray's might
As back to England Mary made her hasty flight.
Upon her sister's mercy she herself did fling,
But royal sibling love, once lost, means not a thing.
For once the giddy taste of power is acquired,
A ruthless savage streak in one is often fired –
For everyone, it seems, intent upon your throne

And in its sure defence you stand or fall alone.
So Mary to a prison cell became a guest
The northern dukes rose up to free her from arrest.
And many were defeated in this futile attempt:
Superior force will treat those weaker with contempt.
The Duke of Norfolk sought sad Mary's hand to wed,
But ended up upon the grim scaffold instead.
That year in France upon St Bartholemew's Day,
A massacre of the Protestants held sway.
Now hapless Mary was condemned without a proper trial:
Whatever truthful plea she made was bound to fail.
Imprisoned for conspiracy for nineteen years,
Unhappy Mary Stuart perceived her worse fears:
That wretched, wretched end for which she most had dread
Now came to pass – beneath the axe she lost her head.
How apt that she who had so many put to death
Should lose, in such injustice, her murd'rous breath.
Elizabeth the Protestant causes supported,
While Catholics abroad did all to have them thwarted.
Both men and money went to help the French king's fight
And also the Catholic Strong League, whose might
Had spread its armies 'cross the whole of Europe's length –
Elizabeth defeats the French with new-found strength.
She also sent an army to assist the Dutch
Throw off the Spanish cruel, intolerant clutch.
The freeing of these countries from Catholic yoke
Was bound the vengeful ire of Spain to sore provoke.
A vast, 'invincible' armada was built by Spain
One hundred and fifty fighting ships move across the main
On orders of Philip II, sailing slow,
With majestic prowess the meddling English to show
No one could spite the pious King of Spain for long:
His mighty fighting force would right such foolish wrong.

It was to be by the proud Duke of Parma's men,
On whose tough veteran soldiers they could all depend.
But doughty Dutch small ships blockade Channel ports
And Spain had to engage alone, without supports.
Yet still the Great Armada sailed towards our shore.
Whatever ships the English had, they procured more,
For only thirty-six small ships formed our defence –
But merchants, nobles and citizens, at their expense,
Provided additional small ships this land to save.
Lords Howard, Hawkins, Frobisher and Drake close watch
    the wave
For threatening sails whose crescent form came proudly on,
While calmly Drake, before his sailor hat would don,
At first insisted in his quiet English way
To end the game of bowls that he'd begun to play.
Then he and all the other doughty sailor men
Came up behind the Spanish ships to harass them.
Against the crowded foe, fireships were blazing sent
And soon their line of battle was completely rent.
Confused and hounded from the rear, the Spanish fled,
Sailing homeward round Scotland's coast in fearful dread.
Their mighty vessels by violent storms were wrecked
And Spanish aims of vengeance thus completely checked.
For few of the invaders would reach home again,
Nor see for evermore the sunlit shores of Spain.
Irish disturbances in this long reign were heated,
The English by the Earl of Tyrone were defeated.
Elizabeth sent Essex, her favourite, to fight,
But in pompous displays he would too much delight.
He was recalled and ired the outraged queen who said,
'Take him away and part him from his foolish head!'
A deed she would regret throughout her lonely life.
Lord Mountjoy now arrived to quell the Irish strife:

The malcontent and Spanish allies were put down
And Ireland cower'd beneath the forces of the crown.
After a long reign of forty-five years she died,
The glory of the age and England's lasting pride.
Elizabeth was vain, fickle, fond of dress,
Too fond of flattery from those who would impress.
She was at times a cruel and cold, cold-hearted queen,
But still the greatest patriot that there had been.
Great grammar schools were founded in her glorious reign
And Raleigh brought 'the dreaded weed' across the main:
Tobacco from Tobago came from far out west,
The India Company, for its rich trading quest,
Received a royal charter for the eastern trade,
While Francis Drake around the world three sailings made.
And brought potatoes back to plant in English soil,
An endless source of food and unremitting toil.

## James I

King James VI of Scotland thus ascends the throne,
The Scottish crown and English crown not now alone:
In peaceful harmony are united at last,
A fragile peace, alas, that was too soon to pass.
For soon religious strife disturbs the kingdom's ease,
Since differing religious views are hard to please.
Conspiracies arise against the Stuart king
By those who would back to the old religion swing.
They tried to place Arabella on England's throne,
But this unwise conspiracy was overthrown.
A gunpowder plot to blow up our parliament
Was just another unsuccessful, ill-judged attempt:
Five kegs of gunpowder were planted ready to light,

But evil deeds seldom ever work out aright.
A missive to Lord Montague betrayed the scheme,
Destroyed the wild conspirators' ambitious dream.
The vaults beneath the House of Lords were searched with care
And foolish Guy Fawkes found with lighting tallows there.
He was arrested and put to death; co-plotters fled
To take up arms against the crown, but soon were dead.
Although their plot would come to naught, its legend lasts:
Each fifth November relived with firework blasts
And bonfires, rockets, and star-like bright flaming flare,
Straw effigies of foolish Fawkes from bonfires stare.
Sir Walter Raleigh sails to the New World, to found
The colony of Virginia for her renown,
Honouring Queen Elizabeth, the Virgin Queen,
One of the greatest women we had ever seen.
She knighted Raleigh for his brave, romantic deed,
Though soon it proved that his colony would not succeed.
But in the reign of James he was imprisoned for
Conspiracy with Lady Stuart, described before.
When Walter Raleigh was in traitor's prison hurled,
He used his time to write a history of the world,
Then was released to search for hidden hoards of gold
That South America concealed within its hold.
His men, however, plundered the settlements of Spain
In their avid, enthusiastic lust for gain.
And so King James − the irate Spanish king to please −
Decided that Walter Raleigh's plunder had to cease,
Sentencing him to death on charges fifteen years old,
So bringing to a close the life of Raleigh bold.
Protestantism was now the realm's religious choice,
The leading divines new reforms began to voice.
They raised a petition to lay before the king,

But he objected, would not concede any such thing.
Instead a new translation of the Bible willed,
Which teams of scholars so marvellously well fulfilled.
The Nonconformists and the Catholics were grieved
That under James no toleration they had received.
Some Puritans to find new lives abroad set sail
And founded settlements in which their views prevail.
These Pilgrim Fathers in America were free
To worship as they wished, and, as we would soon see,
Declared their independence from the British crown,
And so United States they would in freedom found.
Although a scholar, James pedantic was and vain,
By 'divine right of kings' believed that he could reign.
He thought a king could do whatever he desired
And no others' permission would be required.
Self-willed, tyrannical, to rule he so decided
Without a parliament lest they his wish derided.
When parliament decreed such rule against the law,
Their written signed protest he arrogantly tore:
'The liberties of parliament', 'the people's birthright' –
Against these things the wilful James would strenuously fight.
Influenced by his favourites, King James held court:
His favourite, one Robert Carr, was later caught
Involved in poisoning Sir Overbury, who
His role as court advisor would profoundly rue.
The Duke of Buckingham, the king's next favourite,
Whose overbearing ways and pride would outwit
The marriage plans of Charles the Prince of Wales with Spain,
Placing relations with that country under strain.
Prince Charles would later marry Henrietta of France,
And all relations with that state thereby enhance.
Even Sir Francis Bacon, his chief minister,
Would soon also the anger of the court incur –

But not before he wrote his brief and wise essays,
Teaching the king's first son his intellect to raise.
Alas, Prince Henry died when he was but eighteen:
No one can know what future talents might have been.
Bacon, the greatest, wisest, meanest of mankind,
In whom both good and bad, as in us all, we find,
Convicted was of taking bribes, a custom rife,
But for Lord Bacon a blot upon a worthy life.
The king himself of ague died at fifty-nine,
Unswerving in his view that royal rule was divine.
In this long reign the Bible was ably translated
And Napier logarithms invented, always well rated,
Until the modern age when calculators fast
Consigned their lists to something found but in the past.
King James established colonies in Ulster lands
Which, confiscated, were paid for by those wealthy 'grands'
Who bought the new created title of baronet
And what they pay for is really what they get:
True worth and honour sets purchased titles at nought
Beside those won by noble deeds and noble thought.
Those times witnessed great writers: Shakespeare was the best,
Also laconic Bacon, Ben Jonson who blessed
The world with prose and plays that reached the greatest
　　heights –
So rarely soars the human mind in sublime flights,
That we can only marvel at their genius from below,
Whose radiance persists with undiminished glow.
Harvey the circulation of the blood had found,
And Kepler taught that planets go a-whirling round,
While Galileo used the telescope to stare
Into the vast immensity of heaven, where
Some hold the fate of man by music of the spheres
Predetermined is throughout his lasting years.

In time we would outgrow such false beliefs and find
That our destiny lies in the power of man's mind.


## Charles I

When Charles I with pride ascends the British throne
He thought that he – as he'd been taught – could rule alone,
That he could do whatsoever he wished or pleased.
His marriage, his outraged subjects clearly displeased:
He Henrietta wed, daughter of king of France,
A Roman Catholic, in this he took a chance.
Religious turmoils had unsettled previous reigns,
And some feared strongly that he would reverse Protestant
    gains.
Abetted by Duke of Buckingham, his favourite,
Badly the king would parliament often spite.
The shadow of the scaffold cast its eerie shape,
A future which his karma wouldn't let him escape.
More quarrels rose with parliament that won't accede
To arbitrary calls for the money which he'd need.
Advised by Buckingham, the headstrong king dissolved
His parliament – the problem of their thwarting solved.
So Charles endeavoured by tax and enforced loans
To spend the moneys which as king he thought he owns.
Enraged, the people against his taxes loudly complained,
The king's extravagance, alas, was not restrained.
Those who refused to pay these taxes to prison went;
A petition to parliament was quickly sent,
Which to impeach the Duke of Buckingham firmly resolved,
Until the king this second parliament dissolved.
A parliament, the third, the king contrived to tame,
Drew up a petition of rights – of fleeting fame.

For Charles, no sooner had he signed its terms, regretted,
Once more dissolved the parliament, to rule unfettered.
The history lesson which these actions well taught
Is that against real power, words shall count as naught
Since power held and used for reasons right or wrong
Ever gives sanction's stamp to the unflinching strong.
King Charles selected Sir Thomas Wentworth to advise,
Which, like his other choices, was also unwise.
He placed tonnage and poundage on all ports and towns,
A loathsome tax which had most doubtful legal grounds.
John Hampton raised a case against this hated tax,
But fearful of the king, weak judges twist the facts
And ruled the tax was legal, contrary to sense:
Against despotic kings weak judges are no defence.
When despots get away with wrong, they lose their heads
And tear restraining laws into unwelcome shreds.
So Charles resumed his arbitrary solo rule,
For hubris often makes a man act like a fool.
His Star Chamber chased up those who the tax evaded;
His Court of High Commission state religion aided.
Duke Buckingham persuades the king on France to war,
But he was stabbed for discontents he caused before.
In Scottish and the Irish realms more troubles arose,
Resulting from the policies the king had chose –
For Stratford's rule in Ireland proved to be too harsh,
Provoking strong rebellion amidst the mists and marsh.
While Scotland fought all changes to their long-held rites:
Too often differences of faith led but to fights,
Whilst preaching universal love between all men,
A contradiction which no one can long defend.
King Charles assembled parliament yet once again,
The fourth since he began his fraught, tempestuous reign.
But still this parliament would not grant him supplies,

71

In three short weeks the king's slight patience quickly dies.
Once more the parliament is swift dissolved away:
He'd only tolerate those who would him obey.
The Royal Guard by Scotland's army was defeated
And from Newcastle royal soldiers fast retreated.
Disputes between the Scots and English were made well
By both their parliaments, though on the English fell
The costs of keeping Scottish arms on English soil –
But nothing seemed the king's ambitious aims to spoil.
His fifth and long-lived parliament was reassembled,
Which much of previous hated acts and laws dismembered.
Made bold by Scottish arms, it sought to curb the king
And to the nation's grievances more justice bring.
In 1641 the Catholics broke out
In Ireland, and a time of troubles brought about.
Undaunted, Charles still sought to raise by wrongful means
The cash he needs to fund his grandiose wild schemes.
He sought to arrest those who most opposed his plans
And marched upon the House of Commons with his bands,
But found the wanted five absent by prudent design:
This bold attack on English subjects would align
Its members votes to take upon themselves the right
To have command of our armed forces' massive might.
The king refused assent to this restricting law,
So parliamentarians decided to go to war.
The Royalists, as horsemen, 'Cavaliers' were called,
By birth as gentry and noblemen were installed
Within the royal courts, climbing great social heights,
And were with sword and horsemanship well trained for fights.
Supporting parliament were merchants rich from trade
Who London and surrounds their power base had made.
They were ill-disciplined in use of warrior arms
And caused, at first, the Cavaliers no great alarms.

With hair cut short, they were nicknamed 'Roundheads' in
    scorn,
A dull and puritanical plain dress was worn.
At first with skill the Royalists their battles won:
None could, it seems, eclipse the rising royal sun.
The king in person led his armies, who would win
Their battles in the north-west, nor would give in
While they, the better trained, could rout the rabble foe,
But then Cromwell reversed the fight's one-sided flow.
He trained and sternly disciplined his east coast men
Until they could with honour hold their own again.
The English and the Scots desired to curb the king,
Their unified attacks would victory soon bring.
The Royalists in the north met complete defeat,
Yet in the south and west the king could not be beat.
At Newbury against Cromwell the king held fast,
But as the royal cause grew weak, it couldn't last.
In Scotland, although Montrose that cause maintained,
Badly defeated at Selkirk, he lost all that he had gained.
Routed at Naseby, Charles in 1645
Surrendered to the Scots in order to survive.
He hoped his fellow countrymen would him protect,
But that request the Scots, for monies due, reject.
They wished to get the money owing for their aid
And handed Charles to English foes when they were paid.
Imprisoned at Carisbrooke upon the Isle of Wight,
Where he could no longer pursue the royal fight.
In life one thing alone on which you can depend
Is that each pursues their own completely selfish end.
A second period of civil war began
With risings in the east and Kent and Wales, whose plan
Was by the force of arms to aid the royal cause:
This wretched civil war seemed not to know a pause.

The Scots invaded and Royalists marched from the north,
Incurred the Roundheads' harsh and firm resisting wrath.
Fairfax the insurrection near to London swift quelled,
While Cromwell Cavaliers in Wales and the north soon felled.
Behind the Roundheads' back the weak parliament then sought
To reach agreement with King Charles whom once they
    fought.
They feared the rising might the army now could wield,
But ere a treaty could be signed, they had to yield.
So Charles was to Hurst Castle quickly then removed
The strength of strict Roundhead training was well proved.
Next fickle parliament was purged by Colonel Pride:
Only those remained who were on the army's side.
This rump of a parliament now put the king on trial:
A charge of waging a civil war could never fail.
And so the Court of Justice sentenced Charles to death
In 1645 he breathed his last fond breath.
He bravely bore his death and lost his corrupt crown,
For with great fortitude he went to lose his head,
'I go from this to an incorruptible crown,' he said.
Since Charles believed he had the right divine to rule,
He felt he had no need of parliament at all.
A haughty tyrant and despot he soon became,
Forgetting that with sole command too comes sole blame.
In private life he was a father good and kind,
A man more moral and loving we seldom find.
Yet as a king his duplicity brought him down,
For Machiavellian schemes are built on shifting ground
And, once exposed to view, as soon or late they must,
They will destroy all chance of deep and lasting trust.
He was a cultured man of fine artistic taste,
Who Rubens' and Van Dyck's great paintings did embrace.
Van Dyck's large portrait shows his mild and mournful eyes,

Behind, a thoughtful mind of feelings profound lies.
When wilful monarchs have their warring, wanton way,
The more tax their oppressed subjects begrudging pay.
To meet the civil war's uncheckable high cost,
A tax was levied to recoup the rising loss.
Great fortresses were in this civil war destroyed
And many graceful treasures of old churches despoiled.
While emigrations to America were rife,
Fleeing these troubled, tortured times to seek new life,
Until by royal proclamation this was slowed,
Though settlements to West Indies still quietly flowed
To form the first of the colonies in those fair isles,
For hope of peace induces men to search for miles.
Alas, when will men learn that peace resides within,
And he who flees himself can never calmness win,
For only in a heart at peace shall men be free,
And from his own true self no one can ever flee.


## The Commonwealth

When Charles had been beheaded, his son was made the king
Of Scotland and of Ireland, but this did not bring
The crown of England, for the Commons voted away
The office of the king for ever and a day.
Also the House of Lords abolished was as well,
Sounding, it seemed, the old establishment's death knell.
Lord Cromwell marched on Ireland; crushed the royal cause
With merciless severity, without a pause.
All towns that would not yield were stormed and put to death,
Until within a mere nine months no fight was left.
In Scotland for his prince, Montrose most bravely fought,
His capture and his death brought that attempt to naught.

From Ireland back, Cromwell the rebel Scots defeats
And then, when Charles invades, the would-be king he beats.
So Charles escaped to France, losing his chance to rule:
In this escape he showed himself to be no fool.
Disguised in female clothes, he managed to stay free;
Another time as soldiers came, he climbed a tree
And watched them from his perch as they searched hard
    below.
Resistance both in Scotland and in Ireland ebbed low.
In 1651 a very selfish law was made,
Levelled against the rival Dutch rich shipping trade,
Forbidding imports that came from far distant shores,
Except the goods transported in the cargo stores
Of English ships – much to the valiant Dutchmen's rage,
Who would against the English bitter warfare rage.
The English admiral defeats the Dutch at sea
In one of many battles fought so bitterly.
In turn the Dutch defeat the English on the sea,
Determined that they would those trade restrictions free.
Van Tromp carried a broom atop his lofty mast,
'To sweep the avid English from the seas at last!'
Three bitter fights ensued in which Van Tromp was killed
And England thus regained her mighty naval shield.
Much rivalry between the parliament 'The Long'
Or 'Rump' and Cromwell's army, well ordered and strong,
Was ended when Lord Cromwell, with his troops outside,
Into the Commons came, its members to deride.
He stamped his foot, which was a prearranged loud sign
To summon in his troops, who stood in threatening line:
'For shame, you are no parliament, now get you gone,
And take away that empty bauble!' So out was borne
The mace, a symbol of their authority, lost.
The members were from out of the chamber rudely tossed,

A silence fell across their empty ornate room,
And slammed and locked its doors upon its growing gloom.
Lord Cromwell stamped his own authority o'er all the land:
Against such ruthless rule no one dare take a stand.
He opened instead a parliament obedient to his will:
This 'Little' parliament all opposition would still,
For those courageous members who came to object
Unsmiling and insensitive soldiers eject.
The control of all the state returned to army hands,
Fulfilling well Lord Cromwell's strict reforming plans.
As Lord Protector of the Commonwealth he led
New changes to the state which many subjects dread.
He had few friends, yet could upon his troops rely,
Who for their fearless leader were prepared to die.
But Royalists and most republicans did him detest
And parliament his authority would test.
Lord Cromwell, angered, dissolved the parliament again;
The next proposed to crown him king, the throne to gain,
But Cromwell wisely this declined, aware that his men
Would not accept return to what they fought to end.
His son-in-law, Fleetwood, a commonwealth preferred
And to this proposition Cromwell then deferred.
A leader, strong as he was, could not rule alone;
Without support he stands a mortal on his own.
What use is it to order when no one obeys?
He must appear to value men and nature's ways.
In overseas affairs Cromwell dazzled the people's eyes,
With Holland making peace; against proud Spain he vies;
He captures Jamaica and chases pirates away;
The reckless Duke of Tuscany he made to pay
For damage to the English ships and their rich trade.
Returning Spanish galleons became afraid,
For English ships captured them and took their gold

And looted treasures hid within the Spaniards' hold.
In one sea fight sixteen treasure ships of Spain
Were set alight and many sailors burnt or slain:
Within the harbour of Santa Cruz Tenerife
The blazing galleons in crazy circles drift.
Our victorious admiral would not long live to see
His grateful countrymen express their heartfelt glee,
For he would breathe his last as Plymouth Sound was reached.
When English forces Dunkirk's forts and dunes had breached,
The French surrendered Dunkirk to the English hands.
(How future times would come to know those fatal sands!)
His ruthless massacre at Drogheda disclosed
How cruel was Cromwell when he was disposed.
But none could deny how much energy he had,
Nor how decisive, firm, he was when things went bad.
By land and sea at home as well as overseas
He caused the name of England through these victories
To be respected, and added to this nation's glory
Who as a formidable world power changed its story:
To the United Provinces dictating peace,
Causing the Spanish threat by land and sea to cease.
He took revenge on Barbary pirate ships
And seized West Indian isles with tightly grasping grips.
By taking famed Dunkirk upon the Flemish coast,
The French no longer could the gain of Calais boast.
In 1658 the great Protector died,
Richard his grieving second son was by his side.
Although Richard became Protector in his place,
He soon retired to private life, leaving no trace.
On cautious Monk the destiny of England fell,
A general who was perceived as reserved as well.
In secret, Monk wrote to Prince Charles, who in exile
Still tried to plot return to England's throne in style.

So Monk to York his army marched with firm intent,
His steady progress noted by spies where'er he went.
Towards the north John Lambert marched from London Town,
Intent on putting Monk's invading army down.
But he by all his fickle soldiers was deserted,
So Monk to London marched and there his strength asserted:
Disarmed the City and a parliament new raised,
And those who once condemned, Charles the prince now
    praised.
The country, too, declared in favour of the prince,
Replaced the royal arms, removed not too long since.
Prince Charles, restored, declared a general amnesty,
Returned to England 'midst much patriotic glee.
In Cromwell's time, East Indian Company began
To trade with Bengal state in that exotic land.
Thus commenced the growth of English power there,
A chapter of imperial might both harsh and fair.
A post office was here established in this 'reign'
And Jews permitted to reside in these isles again.
This Cromwell was a patron of the arts as well
And fostered blind Milton, who wrote of heaven and hell
In poetry so melodious and so sublime,
Its rich wise words and rhythms roll on throughout all time.


## Charles II

In 1660 Stuarts the English throne reclaimed
And Charles II most popularly acclaimed.
But then neglected the wise advice Clarendon gave:
Unprincipled, faithless, to selfishness a slave,
He went his wanton way with regard to none,
What had been done he sought in time to have undone –

Indemnity acts that he initially had passed –
But would these decrees hold to wipe the slate at last?
The crime of regicide could never be condoned
By loyal sons who afterwards became enthroned.
Even the execution of the guilty few
Could never make amends for crimes the whole world knew.
Most soldiers were disbanded except some five thousand
Who, few in number, nonetheless were dressed more grand
Than Cromwell's plain and puritanical Roundheads
Whose very sight each Cavalier despising dreads.
Against Nonconformists by parliament new acts
Were made which Charles, with the Protestants, backs.
Infanta Catharine of Portugal to wed,
Charles his royal bride along the aisle slowly led:
Two forts in Tangier and in India rich Bombay
And money as a dowry came King Charles's way.
But in that year he sold Dunkirk to France's king,
Which had by Cromwell been acquired – a foolish thing
Which future times would look upon with real regret,
But vain it is on what is done to useless fret.
In part to win complete command of seaborne trade,
Avenge, too, those who had his exile unpleasant made,
Charles plunged into a second war against the Dutch,
Whose fleet just off the Suffolk coast fell in his clutch.
Not only did his brother snatch this victory,
But made the seas for English ships securely free.
Yet in this hour of triumph fell fresh blows of fate:
A time of troubles followed, so sad to relate.
A fearful plague broke out and with his deadly scythe,
The deathly reaper reaped arrears of unpaid tithe.
Great piles of bodies o'erswamped the burial grounds
As on and on the Reaper strode his dreadful rounds.
One hundred thousand souls in London lost their lives,

A fate that often comes to those who crowd in hives,
For in a tight confinéd space diseases spread
As close inhabitants help each to join the dead.
Close on the pestilential disaster came
An awful holocaust of all devouring flame
Which swept the city streets from narrow Pudding Lane
And nothing seemed to stop its wild wide-spreading gain.
So many of the grand old buildings were burnt down
And doleful scenes of desolation spread around.
No one should cling to relics of the ancient past,
Though fondly loved, alas, they can't forever last.
To raise renewal costs from bankers proved too hard:
Most sailors were dismissed and ships kept in their yard.
At which unchecked the vengeful Dutch up Medway sailed,
Set fire to English ships and coastal shores assailed –
Until the peace of Breda brought with it amends
New Amsterdam was ceded from the Dutch, which ends
All conflict with the French and Dutch upon the seas
And English ships again could sail where'er they please.
Next Clarendon would be unjustly banished when
King Charles about him chose unprincipled, weak men:
A Clifford, Arlington and Buckingham as well
As Ashley and a Lauderdale, whose intials spell
A 'Cabal', by which profligate ministers henceforth were
    known
(From such accidents as this has English language grown).
A triple alliance formed in 1668
With Sweden and the Dutch creates a counterweight
To Louis XIV's aggressive policy:
How soon foes friends become from sheer necessity!
The mighty Magna Carta had decreed that none
Without a trial the gauntlet of parliament should run,
But Stuart sovereigns this law oft disregarded,

Kept enemies in prisons for long years close guarded.
So government endorsed Habeas Corpus Act
To bring the spirit of the Magna Carta back.
All prisoners should be tried at once, not tried at leisure,
Their trial should not be long delayed at kingly pleasure.
It is an ancient, natural, inviolate law
That those who go against the people are withstood the more.
The pendulum which tyrants force their way to swing
Soon down upon their heads a counterforce will bring.
The Scottish Covenanters in rebellion rose
When 'gainst great tyranny resisting arms they chose.
Archbishops Sharp and Lauderdale oppressed them sore,
Until incensed and roused they would not stand for more.
Untrained, the insurgents were beat at Pentland Hills,
Then cruel persecution added to their ills.
They murdered Sharp and Persecutor Graham beats,
But this does the story of their forlorn fight completes.
For soon the bastard Duke of Monmouth put them down
And many of the Covenanters went to ground.
As parliament excludes the Catholics entire,
This all too soon incurred King Charles's paternal ire.
For from Prince Charles it would authority deprive,
Which caused the king his wilful parliament to override.
He ruled without a parliament for four long years
Which only added to the people's rising fears
And led to conspiracies by the malcontent
Who, if they had not cause, would soon a cause invent.
One Titus Oates had falsely told of popish plot
Against the life of Charles, and death became the lot
Of Catholics said to conspire against the king:
A false report is such a vile and deadly thing.
Next came the Rye House plot that sought to reinstate
A constitutional sound government: sad to relate

Some minor members added assassination to
The growing list of wilder things they wished to do.
But Monmouth, Russell, Sydney, though thought innocent,
Would find the venging king would not one jot relent.
Lords Russell, Sydney both were tried and put to death,
But Monmouth pardoned was and rapidly he left
For Holland, where he lived for years in lone exile,
Whilst James the Duke of York resumed his life in style,
As Lord High Admiral as he had been before:
Unequal justice all the world must well deplore.
For if a favoured few escape the price of crime,
The rule of law will surely lose all trust in time.
Next called 'Meal Tub Plot' by Dangerfield was framed
Which for reward the Presbyterians, he claimed,
Conspired against the king, but when exposed he said
By Catholic high bribes he'd been by them misled,
Who planned to kill the king to further their own ends:
In troubled times a false report much credence lends.
In 1685 the headstrong king was dead
And of him some bad, some good might well be said.
Upon the bad let history but be the judge,
And of the really good let us not meanly grudge.
It was the age of Newton, Locke and Milton too,
And Dryden; great Divines, to mention but a few.
Extensive trade, and navigation was advanced,
And Duke of York the English navy had enhanced.
The Royal Greenwich Observatory was founded,
The Royal Society first science lore expounded
Which would become in time a home of lasting fame,
Winning itself a shining worldwide name.
The Act of Habeas Corpus was made into a law,
Now none could be at whim imprisoned, as before.

# James II

And so the brother of the late departed king
Ascends the royal throne, a hated, hateful thing,
Since James II was a Catholic alone
Amidst a sea of Protestants which lapped the throne.
Revolts were raised in north and south against his rule;
Argyll had landed on Scotland's coast, but cool
Or no support came to his anti-royal cause –
His capture and his death permitted little pause.
When Monmouth landed in Dorset, the peasants rose:
Against his force the tide of war relentless flows.
At Sedgemouth Monmouth was defeated and swiftly fled,
But was discovered in a ditch and very soon was dead.
Judge Jeffreys pursued his followers with zeal
And at the Bloody Circuit Court enjoyed the kill.
Three hundred souls were put to death, deserved or not –
A cruel judge the west has never yet forgot.
King James would brook no opposition to his will;
His right to rule without a parliament was real:
It was the king's prerogative, he rashly thought.
Dispensing with some penal laws, he sought
Some Catholic army officers to enlist,
Still further his popish-favoured aims persist.
Although he claimed he thought the capable should succeed,
And not be prevented from serving well because of creed,
He set aside the test and wished the law to be changed,
That never more should Catholics feel estranged.
The French Nantes Edict revoked and induced the flight
Of most Protestants to England in growing fright,
Which only added to the tensions over here
Between the two religions, giving grounds for fear.
Those fleeing persecution settled in Spitalfields,

Establishing their silk weaving which great wealth soon yields.
A declaration of indulgence was suspended
And disabilities on Nonconformists ended.
The Quakers and other Dissenters too agreed,
But most held it illegal, nor would they accede.
So James commanded his edict in each church be read,
But seven bishops protesting a revolt lead.
The king put them on trial, but which would him annoy:
They were acquitted, which gave the angry nation joy.
Within two days the queen gave birth to a small son,
Which spurred nobles and clergy to have something done
About this Catholic and autocratic king:
What further inroads to their faith this son might bring?
They wrote to William, Prince of Orange, 'Come to fight!
Defend our faith and freedom and put matters right.'
For William was to Mary, King James's daughter, wed
And seemed a better man to wear our crown instead,
His calm Protestant faith much preferred to popish creed
That served to back King James in word and wilful deed.
He landed with his army close to old Torbay:
He came to save our liberties, the English way,
Securing free election of our parliament
(once set aside by James, an act he would repent).
For now Whig nobles of the west and of the north
Would join Prince William and in support came marching
  forth.
And even Anne, his second daughter, James deserted;
To William's side and rallying cause, was converted.
Bereft of family, with few enough of friends,
Lone James could see no one his haughty rule defends.
His queen with infant child one stormy night did flee
To France, as fearful James then stole away to sea.
He tossed the Seal of State into the Thames in spite,

Thinking no deed without its stamp would be thought right.
Then, captured by some fishermen, to London brought
To William, who his presence most unwelcome thought,
Hinted strongly that James should once again withdraw
And take himself off to another foreign shore.
To aid his swift departure, guards took little pains,
Enabling James to flee to France free of his chains.
King Louis XIV's court received him with warm zeal,
That he might safe and courtly comforts feel.
Thus was the English Revolution bloodlessly won,
Thus was it that a new and sober age begun.


## William and Mary

At first the Prince of Orange was approached to see
If he would please accept the English regency.
But this lesser proposal he would not condone,
Insisting power be rested in himself alone.
So parliament the throne in 1689
Offered to William and Mary and their line.
Amidst rejoicing they became our king and queen:
It was just as if the Catholics had never been.
Protestants could resume their lives, from Rome made free,
The Commons drafted a comprehensive new decree.
The grave offences of King James it fully listed
And reinstated all the rights which he resisted.
The ancient rights of common people were restored,
Allegiance to the monarchy was underscored.
While Scotland did not come under parliamentary sway,
It often acted in almost an equal way,
But restless Ireland, which was under the English crown,
Was by these English laws irrevocably bound.

What was King William's and Queen Mary's right to reign?
She was the daughter, he the son-in-law, 'twas plain,
But Jacobites in Scotland still the Stuarts support
And Viscount Dundee 'gainst King William's army fought,
Winning at Killiecrankie's pass a hollow gain,
For in his hour of victory, Dundee was slain.
So Scotland slowly submits, reluctant swore
An oath of true allegiance to William's law.
MacDonald's chieftain failed to take the oath on time,
Dalrymple in his private spite punished the crime –
Although he knew the failure not to be their fault,
An awful massacre upon their clan was wrought.
The finest of the helpless MacDonald were killed
And any thoughts of rebellion were harshly stilled.
In Ireland civil war broke out, which suited James
In his vain bid to win back his rightful royal claims.
On Londonderry he laid siege which long held out
And still held firm, though starving folk began to doubt.
Until, by ship, along the river came supplies:
All hope that Londonderry would surrender dies.
That siege abandoned, James to Boyne his army led,
But was by William's men defeated with many dead.
Crushed James once more to friendly France in exile went.
His vain attempt to take the throne appeared quite spent.
Next William forced the town of Waterford to fall,
Yet Limerick held out, defying one and all.
But later, when the Irish and their French allies
Were soundly beaten at Auchrim, all their hope dies.
Proud Limerick surrendered and its defenders fled –
This brave brigade of Irishmen was by Louis led.
Success was not all one way, as has oft been said:
The English and the Dutch grand fleets off Beachy Head
Before the Battle of the Boyne defeat found,

But what goes round, again in time oft comes round.
In 1692 the fighting English fleet
On French warships just off The Hague inflict defeat,
Which forced sad James to give up all attempts to gain
The throne and o'er the English folk once more to reign.
But now in his campaign against fair France's king,
For William, slow fate's pendulum began to swing.
In 1695 Namur captured again,
Preventing French conquests of more foreign terrain.
Great loans were raised to meet the expense of these wars
From loyal subjects whose wealth formed untapped stores.
This laid the foundation of growing National Debt,
A legacy that is, alas, still with us yet!
A treaty brought an end to this short war at last:
All troubles, however severe and fraught, do soon pass.
For France, Spain, Germany and Holland now condone
King William's legal right to England's ancient throne.
Two treaties to partition Spanish dominions
Were made with Louis by William – in whose opinions
These lands should not by France be grabbed to her gain
Upon the death of Charles II, king of all Spain.
For Charles no issue had, and France with Spain would be
So powerful as to threaten our liberty,
Also the freedom of the nearby states as well:
What harm such union would have brought us, none
    could tell.
When Charles the Spanish monarch was about to die,
He left his vast estates (King William to defy)
To Louis of France's grandson, Philip of Anjou:
Against this Spanish ploy, what could the English do?
A grand alliance was formed to counter this dire threat
With Austria's Grand Duke, who desired Spain's throne to get.
This caused the war of Spanish Succession to be fought:

'Divide and rule' is what past times have always taught.
In 1694 our good Queen Mary died:
Heartbroken was the king, and grief felt far and wide
Throughout this realm, for she had died without a son,
And so the process of succession new begun.
An Act of Settlement decreed the throne to Anne,
The sister of Queen Mary, which proved a timely plan,
For shortly after this the king fell from his horse:
His troubled reign, which he well served, had run its course.
So in his thirteenth year he died, a bitter blow:
What would the future hold? No one could ever know.
The Bank of England had been founded, a lasting boon:
In future finance it would play a leading tune.
The Chelsea Hospital and Greenwich Palace then
Were formed to care for old and wounded servicemen.
Peter the Great of all Russia to England came
To learn and promote Russia's future growing fame.
The war of Spain's succession was ardently fought,
Success by Marlborough's robust men boldly brought,
In spite of obstacles all round which made it hard
To gain from well-entrenched opponents ev'ry yard,
And from sunrise not 'til midday was Nebel crossed:
The fates of both contestants were in turmoil tossed.
Until shrewd Marlborough had formed across the marsh
An artificial road bridging that terrain harsh,
Leading two charges of his cavalry to win,
Much to the beaten French unbearable chagrin.
The capture of the Rock of Gibraltar by Rooke
The haughty pride of sultry Spain profoundly shook,
While Marlborough with Prince Eugene of Savoy beat
The fleeing French, a further deflating defeat.
But in the fields of Flanders they paid a mounting cost:
The victors more than foes their men in winning lost.

Remember well the frightful name of Flanders fields,
Which would in future years a fouler harvest yields.
Harsh history's hard lessons are too soon forgot,
And on these self-same fields fresh fighting men would rot.


## Queen Anne

The wife of Marlborough imperiously held sway
O'er Anne, but gradually her power ebbed away
As by a Mrs Marsham she was supplemented quite
And was no longer welcome to the royal sight.
It was this Mrs Marsham who had the Whigs replaced,
They were the party for the frequent wars we faced.
Instead the Tories came to take complete command
And Marlborough was set aside on their demand.
The English wanted Archduke Charles as king of Spain,
But when their fought-for choice the emperor became,
It proved almost as undesirable that he should unite
The growing Austrian power with the Spanish might,
Permitting the hated French monarchs o'er Spain to rule:
Against the force of fate, resistance adds more fuel.
So by the Treaty of Utrecht the English must allow
King Philip to have Spain when to events they bow.
Much treasure and much blood had they both shed in war,
But change with changing times is survival's harsh law.
So Philip gave up the claims he had for France's throne,
Instead enjoyed the wealthy Indies for his own.
The manner in which Scottish colony Darien
Had been by King William III, by stroke of pen,
Fast sacrificed because of jealousy between
The English and the rising Dutch, by Scotland was seen
To be against their interests: they passed an act

Which stated they would choose a Scottish king: a pact
Guarding their interests upon Queen Anne's decease –
But such a move was not condoned and had to cease
Because the English wished both realms to firm unite,
Both parliaments be one, a plan of shrewd foresight.
And so one kingdom of Great Britain thus was born,
Preventing Scotland from fair England being torn;
Preventing, too, the crown from passing to the Scots,
Although this did not prevent Bolingbroke's dire plots.
But all in vain, for on Anne's death the English throne
Would pass to Hanoverian heirs, to them alone,
Keeping it in Protestant, not Catholic, hands,
Securing freedom from the Pope our treasured lands.
When good Queen Anne fell ill she sent for loyal men,
Dukes Shrewsbury, Argyle and Somerset, to end
The machinations of bold Bolingbroke with speed,
Who plot for James 'The Old Pretender' to succeed.
But just in time, for Anne at fifty sadly died.
Her gentle disposition was a source of pride
And all her subjects did the 'Good Queen Anne' now mourn,
For in her reign a brilliant literature was born,
With Pope the leading poet, while prose could proudly boast
Both Swift and Addison among the gifted host.


## George I

When George I at fifty-four became our king,
But very few his praises could in truth loud sing.
Awkward was he, and coarse, with foreign ways as well,
'Bout which his subjects would in jesting wit retell.
The Whigs, backing Hanoverian programmes, recalled,
Henceforth in parliament they long in favour ruled.

Rash Bolingbroke and Oxford were by them impeached,
As they were charged the Peace of Utrecht to have reached;
'Twas also suspected that treason they had planned
To set 'Pretender' on the throne – most underhand!
When Bolingbroke fled fast to France to join and aid
The 'Old Pretender', it seemed that the case was made.
But Oxford stood his ground, was from the Tower freed,
When he on trial successfully did plead.
Such was the sympathy for Oxford that 'twas feared
A popular rising of the people would be reared.
The Riot Act was passed to stop unruly mobs,
Though some might argue that it their right to protest robs.
If twelve or more foregathered in one place an hour
And would not go away when asked by those in power,
They were then held to be felons before the law,
On whom the rulers could legitimately wage war.
Rebellions were next raised to back the Pretender's claim,
But the rebel Earl of Mar to swift defeat soon came.
Nithsdale and Forster, Derwentwater quickly too,
At Preston met defeat, these sad but gallant few –
Though Forster with the Lord Nithsdale escaped from jail,
The latter dressed in women's clothes and hiding veil
Supplied by his devoted wife, who took great risk
From under guards' suspicious eyes her lord to whisk.
Derwentwater was beheaded on Tower Hill:
For those who treason try, the state's obliged to kill.
His large estates were taken by the angry crown
To found the Greenwich Hospital, of great renown –
Some good will always come from bad, often by chance!
His cause well lost, the Old Pretender fled to France;
His aide, the Bishop Atterbury, fled abroad
To nurse his wounded pride and pray unto his Lord.
An alliance between Great Britain and fair France,

Germany and Holland which might the peace enhance.
Philip V of Spain, however, broke his vows,
Until Lord Byng's warships shot shells across his bows,
Crushing the Spanish fleet right by the Sicilian shore.
Spain's Philip, forced by this, gave up his plans for war,
Whilst in the north, King Charles of Sweden, France's friend,
Who planned to have invaded Scotland, met his end:
At siege of Frederick's hold he by grapeshot slain,
Which made the chance of his invasion now in vain.
In 1720 there arrived the South Sea scheme
Which promised wealth beyond all wildest avid dream.
The nation's debt, no less, by it would be repaid
And in return they'd secure the South Sea's trade.
Men never learn: what seems too good is rarely true;
What looks at first a joy becomes a woe to rue.
In reckless rush the greedy pay outrageous prices
And pride themselves astute until there comes a crisis.
The Bubble burst and thousands faced financial loss
And into destitution soon were quickly tossed.
There is no market for a piece of worthless pulp;
The only course is: seek a swindling rascal's scalp!
'Cometh the hour, cometh the man', the saying goes,
And turns out true as every great wise thinker knows.
Sir Robert Walpole by his prudent management
Restored the credit of a nation over-spent.
Oh, never more would speculation run so rife!
That was the hope, but was that true in actual life?
At sixty-eight King George suffered a stroke and died
When on a visit to Hanover's countryside.
Within his reign Great Britain with Hanover was united,
But through his lack of English, royal power blighted,
For parliament increased to seven years its term
Which gave it greater time its edicts to confirm.

As George at Cabinet councils did not preside,
It soon became his custom in trust to abide
With what his ministers decided to enact:
They merely told him later of the final fact.
Of course the royal seal had still to be applied,
But on his ministers he totally relied.
The dawn of industry grew brighter, brighter still
When Lombe at Derby built his silk-throwing mill.
When to East India Company a charter was granted,
In Madras, Bombay, Calcutta new trade was planted –
The seeds of growing trade which, once they were full grown,
Would form the greatest empire that the world had known.


## George II

King George II gained the throne at forty-five
With Robert Walpole they the Excise Bill contrived,
But opposition proved so great, it had to go.
At Edinburgh a mob on soldiers stones did throw,
For Captain Porteous, who led the City Guard,
Had hung a man with justice, swift and hard –
A rebel brave who helped a fellow felon free –
And when the mob rose up against this tyranny
The captain bade his City Guard on them to fire,
A course of action that would lead to results most dire.
For Porteous, condemned to death, won late reprieve,
But angry mobs would not at this the matter leave.
They burst into the Tolbooth and Porteous seized by force,
Then fiercely dragged him out and, showing no remorse,
They hanged him high on a dyer's lofty pole.
This act incensed in turn the government as a whole,
Who threatened to demolish Edinburgh's town walls

And deprive that city of its charter, but loud calls
Of many Scottish members in our parliament
Soon made the government its rash decree relent.
And so their ancient privileges the Scots retain,
While for the English new-won union could still remain.
When Charles of Austria dying lay, he left his domains
To Maria Theresa, ignoring nephews' claims.
The English would agree these wise, pragmatic moves,
But Frederick of Prussia strongly disapproves
And with the French Silesia take, an act of war
Which brought the Austrian fraught succession to the fore.
Hungarians to Maria gave their fierce support
And to defend their queen and royal son they fought
Against the greater might of French and German foes.
The British, too, her side in the conflict then chose
And George II led in person, with his son,
The British troops, and soon against the French he won.
This proved to be the last of battles that our king
Would lead to victory and royal glory bring.
The course of wars do not run smooth, and like the tide,
So to and fro the flotsam of both armies ride.
In 1743 the French prevailed
And though the British troops fought splendidly, they failed,
But kept their cool and in good order made retreat –
Few armies keep their heads when faced with dire defeat.
Good discipline instals a sense of calm in face
Of bitter loss, which makes defeat no great disgrace.
The war was ended by the Peace of Aix Chapelle
In 1745 – but who can tell
When peace is made between long-standing, bitter foes,
How long before they would again resume their blows?
With England's army absent, there was much unrest at costs
Of aiding Theresa, brought home these rising losts.

And now the restless Scots chose to reclaim our throne,
For Charles, the 'Young Pretender', had sailed home
And landed in the Highlands where the Scottish chiefs
Rallied around his cause, backing his false beliefs.
He marched to Edinburgh, in Holyrood he dwelt:
Before this popular young prince his nobles knelt.
And these Highlanders then defeated brave Sir John Cope,
A victory that raised still more their soaring hope.
Emboldened by this feat, he next England invades,
And through Carlisle, then further on to Derby braves.
But lacking French support and any English aid,
Turned back towards the north, a slow retreat he made.
But even then at Falkirk, Hawley he'd defeat,
Yet never more could he this victory repeat.
The Duke of Cumberland o'erthrew the Scottish hordes
And yet in spite of bribes of handsome, rich rewards,
Not even the poorest of the poor would Charles betray,
So after many dangers he had to sail away.
Escaping to the continent, sad to reside
Until in Rome the exiled Young Pretender died.
From 1756 'til 1763,
A conflagration from live embers came to be
Smouldering after the Austrian Succession, this meant
Full seven years of war across the continent.
From small disputes in North America there arose
A pretext (where both French and British folks oppose
Each other's boundaries) then spread across the world,
Both anxious that alone their flag should be unfurled –
Especially in India which they both lay claim.
The French thus to the side of Queen Theresa came,
Whilst Britain took the part of Prussia's regal king
With Earl of Chatham leading the political wing.
In India foul Surajah Dowlah with French aid

Captured Calcutta in a fast and furious raid.
One hundred and forty-six, all British prisoners,
In the 'Black Hole of Calcutta' so hideously he inters.
This 'Hole' was only eighteen by fourteen feet wide,
But all the prisoners were crammed packed tight inside.
By morn's first light not more than twenty-three survived,
The rest from suffocation couldn't be revived.
And in revenge, changing his quill pen for sword,
Brave Robert Clive reversed the victory thus scored.
Completely crushed Suraja Dowlah's fighting men,
Confirming that the sword is mightier than the pen.
The British also gained a mighty victory
Over the French at Minden within Germany,
But in revenge the French soon Minorca retook:
For this the Head of Affairs should resign, but shook
Responsibility onto Admiral Byng,
A most disgraceful and most ignoble thing.
Alas, the back-up force sent out was much too small,
No blame would fall on those who caused the loss at all.
None had, as Byng had, served their country brave and well:
But no matter how illustriously one may excel,
When once the fates have chosen what shall be your lot,
There is no saving then. The wretched Byng was shot.
In North America, the British met defeat
From French and Indian forces, a surprise complete,
Near Fort Duquesne in Ohio's thick-set wood –
But British troops reverses such as this withstood.
Never for long would the English men retreat,
But just renew efforts, their enemies to beat.
The French headquarters were at Quebec on a cliff
Which soared above Saint Lawrence's wide river swift.
And fortified most strongly by ten thousand men
Whose task it was this lofty fortress to defend.

On the young General Wolfe fell the lot to take
This stronghold city from the French for England's sake.
So from the further shore he made attempts to land,
But each evaporated like water spilt on sand.
Three weary months were spent without a hope to win
And lesser men by now would have chosen to give in.
But not the English men still raring for more fights:
Now they storm up the soaring Abraham Heights.
Which were unguarded, since no one could ever scale
So steep a slope, and would, if trying, surely fail.
How oft in history we read the unexpected wins!
Thus on a moonless night the brave assault begins.
In boats soft rowed with muffled oars that glide,
The English force landed upon the other side,
And from a little cove they clambered up the steep
As unsuspecting French indulged in unsafe sleep.
At break of day they woke to see the scary sight
Of hostile soldiers standing proud upon the height.
A terrible fight followed, the carnage too was great,
For neither side would their untiring fight abate.
'Twas only when Montcalm, the brave French head, was killed
The furious French attack at last was finally stilled.
But in his very hour of victory Wolfe died,
His mourning officers gathering at his side.
'They run! They run!' went up the distant sounding cry.
'Who runs?' 'The French.' 'Then I a happy man to die!'
Thus gasped brave Wolfe before they buried his body here,
Where he had won his famous victory so dear.
And Canada the British next annexed with speed,
Which by the Peace of Paris France had to concede.
King George II sadly died of heart disease,
So this momentous, eventful reign would cease.
For Death cuts down the high as well as those below:

Even the grandest through death's dark doorway must go.
He was succeeded by his grandson, who at cricket was hit
So hard he died, and never on the throne would sit.
So gentle seems the pleasant English cricket game,
But every ball could injure, badly bruise or lame –
Just like the English polite, disarming smile,
Which hides a hard residue of shrewdness and clever guile!
What other momentous changes occurred
In years before the crowning of King George III?
Then coal was used instead of wood to iron smelt,
Whose long-term benefits would be hereafter felt.
And turnpike gates were established throughout the land
To help finance the maintenance of roadways planned.
In 1753 there was wisely founded
The British Museum, whose artefacts astounded
All those who came curious its rare contents to view
And opened up strange worlds of which they little knew.
While in this reign the first stretch of canal commences,
Heralding wide and future changes – and more expenses.
Walpole was the first prime minister that post to name,
Starting a line of noble men of lasting fame.
Electric leyden jars by scientists were devised,
Whose 'magic' powers caused alarm and all surprised.


## George III

When George III became the next illustrious king,
He chose at once to do a most unusual thing.
In his first speech to the assembled parliament,
Inserted words that showed his own desired intent.
He said he gloried in the name of Britain, then,
Disliking Pitt, replaced his team with other men.

Lord Bute was made prime minister, but still the war
Of seven years continued, though less than before –
For both the British and the French had weary grown
Of fighting on for such a length of time, and to atone
Conclude a peace at Paris in 1763
And then a further welcome peace in Saxony.
By both King Frederick of Prussia and the Queen
Of Austria, Maria Theresa, and strife between
The warring parties seemed at last to reach an end,
For none protracted wars can long or full defend.
Lord Bute became unpopular because he gave
Too many spoils of war to France, the peace to save.
For giving up was ne'er an enduring English trait,
And giving up to France, our foe, was bound to grate.
He was replaced by Granville, a much better choice:
All politicians have to heed the people's voice.
The colonies of North America now claimed
Attention from the British on whom all their ills were blamed.
These far-off colonies were full of Puritans,
Who by their independent ways and thrifty plans
Amassed, from trading, growing hoards of gold,
Making them independent and hence quietly bold.
The doughty Dutch settled along New York's coastline,
While Catholics and Cavaliers southwards incline.
But though of England as the motherland they were proud,
No meddling with their privileges now would be allowed.
Their fight for complete independence was caused by
The imposition of new duties levied by
The British, arbitrarily, without a choice,
Not allowing America's own views to have a voice.
The British deemed it proper the colonists pay
Towards the costs of the late war without their say.
They placed a duty first on stamps and then on tea,

Which was shipped out to distant Boston by the sea.
Disguised as Indian men, the ships were swiftly boarded:
They seized the precious cargo that was dryly hoarded,
To throw them ceremoniously over the side,
Where tea chests sank at once, or float the ebbing tide.
These colonists' just cause by Burke, Fox and Pitt
Vigorously supported, yet nought came of it,
For obstinately the king their warning would not heed
And felt repressive measures were the pressing need.
At Philadelphia next a Union congress met
And against such unfair taxes all minds were firmly set.
The British and Americans would soon collide
When first a victory fell to the Union side.
Thirteen far colonies became the United States;
Each side henceforth would fearless face their separate fates.
George Washington their Union commander became
(He as first president would later rise to fame).
The first initial encounter came at Bunkers Hill
Where Royalists the battle won – a bitter pill.
The States their independence declaration swore
And broke all allegiance to the crown for ever more.
The surrender of Burgoyne's army to General Yates
And Franklin's letters induced the French to join the States
To fight the English, joined too by the Dutch and Spain,
With secret hopes no doubt of some eventual gain.
Lord Chatham, once an ally, rose from his sickbed
Speaking against those who joined our foes – and then
    dropped dead.
All in the House of Commons praised his fiery speech,
But history oft has this lesson still to teach:
Whenever stronger nations rule by force, the weak,
As soon as they gain strength, full freedom seek,
And to this end they will those enemies embrace

Who claim to share their hatred of the ruling race.
From Boston British troops withdrew, New York regained,
And still against invasions Canada retained.
George Washington at Brandywine met with defeat,
While fresh fighting was opened up by Britain's fleet.
Fights ebbed and flowed just like the wild and restless seas:
St Pierre, Dominica, Miguilon France captured with ease;
While Britain Pondicherry captured from the French;
In turn St Vincent, Granada from us they wrench.
The Spanish too besieged Gibraltar, but in vain,
For Rodney's fleet broke up their siege and eased the strain.
But when Cornwallis surrendered his fewer men
To Washington, the war at last drew to an end.
Just as his maiden speech by William Pitt was made,
The fatal cards of future times were deftly played.
The independence of the States was recognised
By treaties at Versailles – a compromise devised,
While Canada remained within Great Britain's sway,
Proving a loyal, steadfast friend to this very day.
As often comes in times of turmoil and great change,
Upheavals spread beyond the battlefield's wide range:
Industrial innovations that would shape the age;
Wedgwood's fine earthenware new painted became the rage;
The spinner's jenny, whose frames and mule made spinning
    fast,
In face of which the cottage craft could not long last.
John Wilkes from the Commons for his libel was expelled:
Too often are the great by arrogance swift felled.
Brave Captain Cook set sail across the southern main,
Discovered Australia's remote and dry terrain –
A find that added to England's imperial might,
Which annexation proved for good if not by right.
On Sandwich Islands, Cook was killed in '79:

Those who great dangers seek so often dangers find.
But such adventures lure, and hidden dangers hide,
For men will always live a risky life from pride.
In 1772 the Spanish crown conceded
That Britain held the Falkland Isles, and war receded:
Holds them by right, which ever since she would defend
Against false claims which later states in greed pretend.
King's Bench decides that slaves who landed on Britain's shore
Shall gain their freedom and be abject slaves no more.
Here Sunday schools were by Rawkes and others newly
    founded;
At Spithead *Royal George* capsized and many drowned.
For seven years 'twas calm before the storm clouds rocked
Fair France, when revolution there the whole world shocked.
Three causes fired the spirit of the people's ire:
Oppression by the ruling classes, and Voltaire's fire
And Rousseau's pen; excesses by the royal court
Which, as the people starved, engaged in idle sport –
And when the poor did plead for just their daily bread,
The queen replied, 'Give them all fancy cakes instead!'
But once the angry mob to bitter fury roused,
Not easily was the fierce conflagration doused.
The pendulum of sullen suffering soon swings,
And Madame Guillotine more murd'rous sings.
When the Bastille fell and was fired with bitter flames,
Most nobles were beheaded to pay for their grave shames.
From north to south blood shed and awful woe prevailed
And nothing would, it seemed, this vengeful ire curtail.
King Louis and Marie Antoinette his queen were led
To Madame Guillotine to lose each royal head.
A reign of terror swept across the frightened land:
None could escape the pitiless accusers' hand.
Even some leaders of the revolution killed,

Whenever fickle doubt or growing envy willed.
All kingdoms round this bloody pit that once was France
Gathered their troops to quell the mob's macabre dance.
As often is the case, events produce the man
Almost as if this was some neat predestined plan:
Napoleon Bonaparte arose to take control,
Across all hostile Europe with fearful ease to roll.
He shook the foundations of empires and frail states –
One wilful man of destiny would seal their fates.
He had risen through the ranks by his ability
And his astute command of strong artillery.
The royal city of Toulon by cannon he defeated
And by grateful France his brave swift capture was fêted.
After the revolution he took over affairs
And swept away the mounting sense of dire despairs.
At the Palace of Tuileries with grapeshot fire
He caused the National Guard in panic to retire.
So saved the French Directory from murd'rous mob,
And when he married Josephine he won the job
Of taking full command in Italy's war, where
The might of Austria and her allies he humbled there.
Against France, Pitt the Younger urged England to war,
But Spain joined France and Holland (friendly allies before).
While overseas the steadfast British navy won,
Causing these foes to rue the war they had begun.
Lord Howe decisively would thrash the bold Brest fleet
And off green Cape St Vincent Spain's ships met defeat,
While from the Dutch the Cape of Good Hope was
     swiftly seized,
The news of which the whole of England greatly pleased.
Winning against these three most hostile warrior foes
Confirmed the strength of naval might our leaders chose,
Yet Spithead sailors mutinied, asking for better pay

And better treatment, but, soon pacified, gave way.
But at Nore they seized their ships and blocked the Thames,
On which the wealth of London Port so much depends.
They would not yield, so government forces o'ercome
Those sailors: hanged their captured leaders, every one.
In this same year brave Admiral Duncan would gain
A glorious victory off Camper Town again,
Against the Dutch, whose fighting ships a match were not
And rued the day that they with France and Spain did plot.
Fierce France, sore jealous of British power in the east,
At once Napoleon's Hussars into Egypt did unleash
In order to reduce the growing British might
And aid the Egyptians if the British they would fight,
To snatch the prize of India from Great Britain's hands
And place the flag of France instead across those lands.
Although Napoleon all Egypt snatched for a while,
His fleet, destroyed in the Battle of the Nile
By Nelson – meant he had to lead his men by land
To Palestine, across the hot Arabian sand.
Which was defended bravely by fierce British fire,
Forcing the French foiled leader to alone retire,
Without his men, to France – where he was consul made:
Despite defeat, great men often emerge unflayed!
In Eire discontent fanned by French aid broke out
Into an open rebellion, which General Lake would rout.
After defeat the French further invasions made
And in their folly, they a losing hand had played:
At Killala Bay forced to surrender up their men.
By Act of Union Britain hoped their claims would end,
Yet history has ever taught that freedom's lure
Is that which unquenched will always long endure.
Henceforth England and Eire in parliament united,
A scheme with which not everyone remained delighted.

When Pitt proposed that Catholics should be emancipated,
The king's opposition was not anticipated.
When failure came, Pitt chose with honour to retire,
All politicians soon of such inaction tire –
And he agreed when soon he was recalled to rule,
Directing the affairs of state with reason cool
Until his death, but not before he sent the fleet
The armed neutrality of Baltic states to beat.
For Sweden, Denmark and Russia all our searching stopped
Of neutral ships, which with the Danes' embargo flopped.
When Danes tried to keep the British from the Sound,
Lord Nelson, breaking through, his naval guns hard pound,
Destroying there the Danish fleet, which brought to end
All hostilities, since no more they could depend
On Russia, whose Emperor Paul was timely killed,
Assassinated before his plans could be fulfilled.
The British army too recovered its reputation
By throwing out of Egypt, that long-coveted nation,
The army which Napoleon had earlier abandoned there.
But they lost the leader of their landing party, where
He died from fatal wounds and never saw regained
The vital lands of Egypt, nor his goals attained.
Great Britain, France, with Spain and Holland tired of war,
Suspended hostilities, peace at Amiens they swore.
Napoleon's new conquests Britain restored, but it would keep
Ceylon and Trinidad: thus France would come off cheap,
For she could hold onto her empire's fresh gains
And hold the greater part of Italy in chains
With Belgium, Holland: this treaty appeared one-sided,
Cool Britain would her turn await; calmly abided,
Letting proud Bonaparte become consul for life.
Soon French and British deep distrust revived fresh strife:
When Pitt resumed office, proud Bonaparte became

A self-crowned emperor to glorify his name.
Prepared wild plans Great Britain to invade,
Which Nelson's victory at Trafalgar put paid.
In this same year Napoleon's troops the Austrians crushed;
Prussia he later humbled and onward thrusted.
Here Pitt and Fox both died, exhausted by their toil,
As they the tyrant's wild ambitions sought to foil.
Lord Grenville formed a ministry of the best men
On whose fine talents our long future would depend.
They passed a law forbidding British ships to trade
In the transport of slaves, which would our state degrade.
Napoleon swore he would wage war on any state
That traded with the English, to which we retaliate,
Insisting that no neutral state should trade with France,
Though this did not curtail Napoleon's swift advance.
He placed his brothers on Europe's new-conquered thrones,
Preserves his line upon all lands that he now owns.
When Copenhagen he shelled hard, the British seized
The large Dutch fleet and so invasion dangers eased,
Stopping them falling in French hands to match our might,
For on the seas we had won every naval fight.
In India Wellesley pursued a fine career
Which showed the world that British troops would know
    no fear.
He strengthened British fame and power in the east:
His greatest victory at Assaye brought release,
Vanquishing the Maharattas whose fighting ceased,
While British influences with victory increased.
Napoleon forced the Spanish king to abdicate,
A foolish move that would in time decide his fate.
He placed his brother Joseph on the Spanish throne
And all of Spain gave vent to one long anguished groan.
Tumult and riots bloodied streets with wild protests

Which cease not, when crushed by French force and harsh
  arrests.
Great Britain heeded the anxious appeals by Spaniards made
And sent an army to give them urgently needed aid.
Sir Arthur Wellesley at Vimiera did rout
The French, but superiors decided to let them out.
They left from Portugal with all their spoils of war;
Brave Wellesley was unfairly recalled and Moore
Was sent to take his place, but he too far advanced
And, finding Napoleon with greater force, chanced
From Burgos to retreat, but he was fast pursued,
So turned to face his foe and battle fierce renewed.
There at Coronna, Sir John Moore when winning died,
His bravery acknowledged on every side.
His gallant enemy Soult raised a monument
Upon the spot where his last breath in pain he spent.
Napoleon departs Spain when Austrians made new threats;
He crushed them at Wagram so none would him forget.
But Wellesley had landed and drove the Frenchmen out
And cleared them from Oporto, Marshal Victor's forces rout.
For these great gains Wellesley Viscount Wellington was made,
The only name of whom Napoleon would become afraid.
There followed many British victories, whose gain
Was to drive out the French from all the rest of Spain.
They were also pursued across the Pyrenees,
With British standards planted on French soil with ease.
Napoleon, flushed with pride, with Europe at his feet,
Now marched his men on Moscow, hoping to repeat
His rapid, splendid conquests o'er that unending land.
Thus mounting hubris made him play his losing hand:
His brilliant star of glory was now on the wane
And only audacious wins might his fading fame regain.
(But as in times to come, men's gambles, however bold,

Cannot defeat the Russian steppes and bitter cold.)
Against advice, he marched five hundred thousand men
Towards the ancient capital of Moscow, then
His battle-weary troops met but a blazing pyre:
The Russians burnt their city down and then retire.
Napoleon, faced with an empty burning shell,
Realised his hopes of plunder had been dashed as well.
And so began the long retreat, painful and slow:
Unable to defeat the deep Russian winter snow,
Four-fifths of that great army perished on that march
From cold and hunger, across a land arid and parched.
Around his battered troops the jackals of his foes
Soon gathered, sensing their wounded, dying throes.
Combined, the Russian, Austrian and Prussian armies meet,
Inflict upon Napoleon's men savage defeat.
And six months on, by Wellington, Soult's army fell,
Hemmed in between the Russian hell and British shell.
The victors marched into the heart of Paris, where
At Fontainbleau Napoleon abdicated there,
Exiled to Elba in comfort, but on his own,
While Louis XVIII now ascends the vacant throne.
Another war with the Americans arose
When Britain claimed the right to search whene'er she chose
Their ships for seamen to serve in the British fleet,
And other various disputes which neither meet.
To conquer Canada the Americans fail,
And on the seas they bravely fought to no avail.
In fifteen minutes the smaller *Shannon* proved her might
And beat the larger Americans in fight.
This distant war was ended by the Peace of Ghent:
What if these bitter battles otherwise had went?
In mainland England at this time the news was sad,
For George III, the king, alas became quite mad.

For nine long years, the regent Prince of Wales would rule,
A fun-loving dandy prince no one could mind at all.
Much progress was achieved in George III's great reign:
Mail coaches first ran between London and Bristol main;
*The Times* began its long and lauded fine career –
Still every day its new and forthright views appear.
Steam engines were applied to spinning cotton thread,
And weaving looms, in spite of doubts, went ahead.
Here Warren Hastings was before the Lords impeached;
Against the trade in slaves Mr Wilberforce well preached;
Dr Jenner's vaccinations first began to fight
The dread cow-pox, and London lit with first gas light.
The Regency was noted for elegance and style:
Its houses, gardens and town squares soon all beguile
And Brighton Pavilion the coast its charms adorn,
Converting with panache all those who came to scorn.
The British premier Spencer Percival was shot
By Bellingham, a merchant who only hardship got
When ruined because the war with France had lasted so
    long –
But still it's never right to answer wrong with wrong.
And, even worse, came news Napoleon had escaped
From Elba and in France campaigns of war now shaped.
Again Napoleon Bonaparte ascended the throne
As Louis XVIII fled, letting him rule alone.
The allied powers war against their foe declared,
An aim quite firm for which no effort would be spared.
In Belgium, men whom Wellington and Blücher led
Towards their foe with firm determination sped.
But Napoleon, to split the allied armies, beat
The Blücher forces, which tactically retreat.
Yet Ney could not dislodge the British from Quatre Bras,
Though they by Blücher's retreat had come too far.

In order to unite with Blücher, British too,
Fell back towards a ridge in front of Waterloo.
While cool Napoleon opposite them took command,
Torrents of rain fell down to soak the battle land –
And still it rained as fight commenced that fateful day.
To breach the English square, French cannon thickly spray
Their famous cavalry fast charged in, but all in vain
For British infantry repelled them time again.
And so a bloody hand-to-hand conflict was fought
Until at seven was heard the Prussian guns retort:
For late, at last, Blücher hastened his support.
A splendid charge of the Old Guard then came to naught
As British bayonets repulsed their brave attack.
Napoleon, knowing that all was lost, fell back,
Began his final slow retreat which was fiercely hounded
By Prussian troops as all his great ambitions floundered.
Surrendered he himself again into the British care
And to remote St Helena was banished, where
In 1821 this warrior slowly died,
A hated wrecker yet respected on ev'ry side.
The British so admired their foe, they his body gave
To France that he might have a hero's fitting grave.
Distress followed on cessation of the long war:
Returning soldiers found things not as once before.
The importation of all corn and grain was banned;
With wages low, soldiers found jobs overmanned
And prices due to scarcities were soaring high.
It seemed an angry revolution drew nigh.
Although in fear a Riot Act was passed at speed,
Mass meetings held in Manchester paid no heed.
But soon a massacre by soldiers (dubbed 'Peterloo')
This movement quelled, and first attempts at reform too:
A precedent which would in distant future years

Bring late fairness for all, allaying needless fears.
King George III in 1820 sadly died,
A once great king who later was his mind denied.
His lengthy reign had seen the most momentous change
When frequent wars and brave explorers far range:
The lure of trade and gold such rovers always attract!
Parry through the Barrow Straits voyaged both there and
    back,
While Ross and Franklin did the North-West Passage find:
There is no limit to a restless, questing mind!
Lord Exmond made a daring sea raid on Algiers
And filled the murd'rous pirates there with such fears
That they were forced to stop in Christian slaves to trade.


## George IV

After nine years the regent king was at last made,
As George IV was ceremoniously late crowned.
At sixty-eight he was by personal debts fast bound
Obliged he had to accept dull Caroline as queen:
A more unhappy marriage was seldom seen.
For misconduct she was unfairly brought to trial;
The king, to get his way, was deaf to her denial.
Unfaithful George did all he could to make them part,
Which caused his wretched wife to die of broken heart.
This made him more disliked in England, where such spite
To the fair-minded appeared unjust and far from right.
But Scots and Irish warmly greeted their visiting king,
As if he'd done no such wicked and awful thing.
Yet public anger from past riots had not died
A conspiracy to kill the Cabinet was tried
When at a fine state dinner they sat side by side.

The Cato Street conspirator, one Thistlewood,
Was caught and executed before his action stood.
Outrages on the British Settlements caused war
In distant Burma, where it was not long before
Sir Archibald Campbell captured Rangoon that year,
And soon Aragon province did Morrison make clear.
Lord Liverpool was forced by an epileptic fit
To retire as premier and his high office quit.
The new prime minister, Canning, the cause of Greece
Against oppressing Turks would champion without cease.
Lord Byron, too, set out to aid their freedom fight
Until at Missalonghi lost life's illustrious light.
Great Britain, France and Russia independence insist
For Greece – though still the Turkish forces fierce resist,
Until our Admiral Codrington sails to beat
The combined, Turkish and Egyptian hostile fleet.
Old Greece became a kingdom free of Turkish rule:
Without aid this would never come about at all.
When Wellington was by the people's will removed,
New liberties were granted as laws improved.
Lord John Russell the unfair test put an end
So that discrimination could no more depend
On parliament to keep the Catholics oppressed,
Which Daniel O'Connor had long persistently pressed.
The profligate and selfish king, as all must, dies:
For kings and commoners alike, their time soon flies.
In 1825 wild speculation flared;
The banks most payments stopped, few merchantmen were
    spared.
And first of voyages made to far-flung India by steam,
While Stephenson's steam rocket, no more a distant dream,
Between Stockton and Darlington people conveyed
At speeds not felt before, and many were afraid.

This had far-reaching impact on the lives of future men,
Whose travels on horse-drawn power would less depend.


## William IV

King William, called the sailor king, began his reign
As Europe by crisis was racked yet once again.
The continental monarchs used their fighting men
(Against such might the poor could not themselves defend)
To take away their subjects' precious liberties,
A policy that only served so many to displease.
Harsh laws in France against the freedom of the press
More rapidly increased the mounting social unrest
That ended in another frightening French revolt
And Charles X was driven out – a mild result
When one reflects how bloody was unrest before.
The ruling clique gave little thought toward the poor
And through revolt Belgium from Holland broke away,
While in Brunswick the people against their duke held sway
And Polish risings caused them with Russia to merge:
All round the world the tides of discontent wild surge.
Even the hapless Emperor of Brazil went,
Nor in more stable England was the fury spent.
The people demanded reform with one united voice,
But Wellington, who found no favour in their choice,
Resigned and left the governing up to Lord Grey,
Who with a Whig majority would win the day –
But not before the Lords flung out the hated Bill
Which sought reforms: this caused riots, which boded ill.
Such was the swell of anger that it caused much fear:
A French-style revolution seemed, alas, too near.
So Wellington's one hundred peers gave up their seat

To leave the House and thus contrive a wise defeat.
In 1832 the Reform Bill was passed
And brought in wider franchises which soon caught on fast,
For Scotland and Ireland too reformed their ways
And many hoped this was the dawn of better days.
Soon came the abolition of the trade in slaves,
For which kind Wilberforce the wrath of merchants braves.
And then were passed humane reforming Factory Acts
Which under-aged employment's harsh long hours attacks.
A Poor Law too was passed which now withdrew all aid
Unless the poor in workhouses with labour paid.
New Municipal Corporation Acts permit
The ratepayers and freemen to elect as fit
Chief magistrates from themselves as they would decide,
And Nonconformist priests could marry groom and bride
In their own chapels, and record their births and deaths.
Thus after foreign shocks our rulers drew deep breaths
And to domestic issues wisely well attend,
Thus continental revolutions off they fend.
For seven most welcome years England enjoyed safe peace
And hoped in vain these calmer times would never cease.
At Windsor Castle William died at seventy-two,
Incompetent, but full of charm and pleasure too:
Critics will carp, whichever way one's life is spent.
Ascends the throne young Victoria, Princess of Kent,
In William's time the fast expanding railway ran
Through to the Port of Liverpool – a clever plan
That brought in bulk the goods of Manchester to sea
Where they to all the world could fast exported be.
Captain John Rose King William Land found as well,
Discovering where the true magnetic pole true fell:
An all-important find for all a sea-faring crew
Who their position could pinpoint more true.

## Victoria

Ascends the throne young Victoria, Princess of Kent,
Whose formative young years in preparation are spent.
A jewel on the British throne that brightly glows,
Beneath whose rule the empire yet still wider grows.
Victoria, eighteen years of age, had been well trained
And when she first met with her council was not strained,
But by her dignity and gentle manners won
The love and steadfast loyalty of everyone.
She said she placed reliance on the wisdom of this
Her parliament and on her people's love; her wish
Always to promote happiness and welfare for
All classes of her people: she was prepared for
By her devoted mother, and, education
Designed to help her serve this mighty, far-flung nation.
In 1840 she charming Prince Albert wed,
Who helped her wisely rule the vast empire she led.
He was of noble character and lofty aim
And everyone did their union most joyously acclaim.
The Prince Consort devoted himself to serve his Queen
And as a model couple they by all were seen.
The value of family life inspired her realm,
All felt secure and safe with Victoria at the helm.
The prince encouraged industry and supported art:
In setting a fine example he more than played his part.
Alas, good things don't last, and his sudden, premature death
Left all the nation and his grieving queen bereft.
Indifferent to human hopes and human love,
The scythe of unkind death sweeps down from high above.
In distant Canada a grave revolt arose
Against home rule, but was suppressed and brought to close,
And when its two distinct provinces were next united

With Ottawa, the capital, they seemed delighted.
But at this time in England too, unrest was great,
For two bad winters, high-priced food, low wages create
A starving, suffering poor which fed the Chartists' fight
For the repeal of the Corn Laws, against the might
Of owners of the land who protection insist
As they against all change continue to resist.
The Chartists planned a meeting next in London Town:
In order to preserve the peace, some troops them surround;
Two hundred citizens enroll to keep the peace;
Against such odds the Chartists' threats of force soon cease.
A band of Welsh rebels disguised in female dress
Against turnpikes did their rising anger fierce express:
Pulled down a goodly number of the toll gates there
Whose constant charges to the poor seemed most unfair.
The hated Corn Laws were attacked which kept prices high
When they all foreign corn free access deny.
John Bright and Richard Cobden fought to win this end
To which John Peel his once-reluctant aid did lend.
The failure of potato crops that Ireland blighted
A prudent change of mind on these Corn Laws incited.
That awful blight and fearful famine many kill,
Those Irish memories of dire times haunt them still.
So many Irish had to leave their cherished home
In search of work and food, the wide, wide world to roam.
At last ten million pounds the British gave as aid,
A generous relief which later was downplayed
By those who sought to break away from England's rule,
Preferring to portray us as remote and cruel.
In England, too, the peasants suffered much distress,
Although their general suffering was much less:
When Peel the hated Corn Laws annulled, then cheaper food
Increased, and so defused this country's hostile mood.

Yet nothing ever comes without a price to pay,
And imposed income tax persists until today.
Since then, this country ever more prosperous grew:
Most were well taught and fed, not just the richest few.
A war with China rose when opium trades they banned
And for that trade and greed an unjust war began.
Our soldiers captured Canton, forcing China cede
Hong Kong with its two ports, and all expense concede,
Defraying Britain's costs of this immoral war –
A chapter of our history we should deplore.
Yet fragile peace enforced by arms could not prevail
And war resumed until our troops Peking assail.
Once more the Chinese, losing, would Kowloon to England
    yield,
Which, opposite Hong Kong, that port yet larger build.
When war broke out between Egypt and fierce Turkey,
It interfered with England's trade in the Black Sea,
So England joined in the fray, shelling Acre and Beirut.
Soon both Egyptians and the Turks cease to shoot,
And signed a treaty where Mohamet Ali could rule:
Egyptian ire and tension then began to cool.
The Afghan Wars, the Sikhs' Mahrattas Wars were won,
An Indian mutiny put down by the cold gun.
In 1854 the Crimean War broke out
When great imperial Russia sought Turkey to rout
And found pretexts to start the war, 'Christians to save
From Turkish rule', but for yet other spoils did crave:
They wished to seize Constantinople and reach the Med,
A move which both the watching French and English dread.
And so the combined armies of British and French
Swiftly the hope of victory from Russia did wrench.
The French and English, shoulder to shoulder, irresistible were,
Although they many deaths and casualties incur.

Sebastopol invested, the battle of Alma gained,
The hardened Allied Forces across the river strained.
In face of deadly Russian artillery fire
Our cavalrymen charged and braved the guns entire,
A brilliant, daring and glorious episode
That gave renown to all who through death's valley rode.
So brave the Light Brigade who fought the guns so well,
Who steadfast kept their charge though comrades around
    them fell.
But then the awful freezing Russian snow descends
And all the Allies' brave advance in torment ends.
The soldiers had no food, were only lightly clad,
Knee-deep in foul trenches crouched, hungry and sad:
As cholera, that dreadful, deadly scourge, broke out,
The dead and dying were like leaves strewn round about.
At home concern for the plight of these troops arose:
Why had they not food nor warmer winter clothes?
That prime minister on whose watch came those disgraces,
Lord Aberdeen, resigned and Palmerston him replaces,
As future times repeated the folly and the cost
Of fighting Russian steppes 'midst winter's snow and frost.
Not all indifferent to fighting forces were,
For Florence Nightingale our nation's consciences stir
To nurse the wounded and bring food to starving men,
Providing clean, light wards on which they could depend
To help them heal war wounds and no infections catch,
And in the end our troops for Russia were a match.
Sebastopol was taken and the Crimean War
Was ended by treaties, where all conquests they restore.
All navigation on the Danube would be free,
But to our national debt was added thirty-three
More millions sterling than we had to bear before:
There never are unscarred winners in any war.

When Southern states seceded from the United States,
They on the supply of cheap cotton shut the gates.
Their civil war added to the cotton mills' distress
While British pirates preyed on the Southern states no less –
For which, when war concludes, Great Britain had to pay
Reparations for her piratical affray.
By 1865 Lord Palmerston had died,
Earl Russell the prime minister became and soon applied
His government (with Gladstone's and Disraeli's aid)
To widened franchise, and a second Reform Bill made,
Thus many more made voters, with more votes for towns:
A fairer voice across both town and country sounds.
Irish Protestant churches were disestablished too:
Religion should not be enforced by just the few.
In education too reforms now came to be
Until good education would to all be free.
While all the British lands north of America
United were as Dominion of Canada,
Except Newfoundland, which alone preferred to stay.
Earlier the punitive Abyssinian War held sway
But was resolved when Britain's army proved its worth.
Elsewhere, alas, of dire conflict there was no dearth.
The French and Germans entered into a war most fraught;
The French completely defeated were, though fiercely they
    fought.
Napoleon III a prisoner taken,
The French Empire was to its proud foundations shaken
And fell apart – and from its fall a republic arose,
Bringing this hopeless war to a disgraceful close.
In England secret voting was secured by law,
Which put an end to undue pressures that came before.
In Africa the fierce Ashanti War began:
Koffee Calalilli on British protected land

Marched in, defeated the Fantees but our ire incites,
Our men his capital captures and end the fights.
King Koffee heavy compensation had to pay.
At home the Liberals with Gladstone lost the day
The Conservative Disraeli now taking charge,
With England becoming more involved in wars at large –
For old and bitter foes Russia, Turkey fights
And England intervened to put these wrongs to rights.
Between the Russians and the Turks this dreadful war
Dismembered Turkey, which less land held than before:
Three smaller states sliced off, Grecian frontiers revised
When Britain with Allied powers new maps devised
In order to prevent fresh wars; firm guarantees
From Britain to the Turks stifle further hostile sprees.
Any such would by Britain be strongly firmly met
And in return our flag on Cyprus we could set.
In Zululand and fierce Afghanistan we fought:
A vast and far-flung empire is oft with troubles wrought.
Arabi Pasha in Egypt revolt raises,
Deposed the Khedive, assumes control in days
'Til Admiral Seymour Khartoum shelled; by land
Brave General Wolseley quickly routs the rebel band.
Arabi, taken prisoner, to Ceylon sent
To live in exile, his last days in leisure spent.
We English, then, with honour treated the foes we beat
(Alas seldom would others such respect repeat).
A humane way of treating old and worthy foes!
The British next the Khedive's restoration chose,
Reformed his army with British officers now in charge
To maintain order in Egyptian lands at large.
A British financial adviser was there implanted
Without whose wise consent no fiscal schemes were granted.
Effectively the British rules that ancient realm,

But with a native figurehead set at the helm.
Arabs from Sudan soon Egypt sought to invade,
But were defeated and to Gordon peace moves made.
Then at Khartoum he was besieged and put to death;
Too late, Lord Wolseley with ten thousand men left,
But on his way the rebels he defeated, where
The desert stretched its blood-soaked sand alone and bare.
So fiercely had the Mahdi fought that there they slew
The generals Stewart and Burnsley, others too.
Though General Wilson's army steamed up the Nile,
Khartoum surrounded, already lost, made help futile.
So he withdrew his force back to Egypt's far north,
But thirteen years thereafter, Kitchener set forth,
Destroying the Khalifa forces, retook Sudan,
Securing Egypt's interests throughout that land.
This firm intention never to give up the fight
Did more than anything to show our lasting might.
At home Gladstone made new reforms on votes and seats
And greater franchises he for most men completes.
A separate Secretary for Scotland was created
Good Gladstone crofters' poor conditions long debated.
Soon after laws were passed which met their just complaints
And freed them from unfair conditions and restraints.
But his proposed Irish home rule was only met
With opposition, for the time was not right yet.
So Gladstone briefly left the political stage,
Returning his home rule campaign again to wage.
Frustrated by the Lords; appeals to one and all:
The time was still not ripe, leading to his downfall.
A wise and noble cause whose failure brought no shame.
Lord Salisbury once more prime minister became,
Extends local government's growing powers,
Bringing control down from the ivory towers.

Abroad, the British Burma soon annex outright:
Against superior guns the Burmese could not fight.
By June of 1887 our queen had reigned
For fifty glorious years, so with joy, and well acclaimed,
The empire celebrated her Golden Jubilee
Which filled her subjects' hearts with love and loyalty.
Vast crowds with joy line deep the grand procession's way,
(Intent on celebrating this momentous day.)
Which wound on to Westminster Abbey, where with pride
The queen and court with heads of empire at her side
Gave her thanksgiving – all hoping she would long reign
And, like a steadfast beacon, in changing times remain.
India had twenty-five thousand prisoners freed,
A cause for celebration by their kin indeed!
Although a brilliant affair, that Jubilee was less
As great as her Diamond Jubilee's shining success.
In April 1900, our queen to Ireland went
And three welcoming, joyous weeks there happily spent.
Warm-hearted were the crowds which put new life in her,
But not for long can mortals their last sleep defer.
For in the year to come, alas, the queen would die
And thus a glorious age of triumph would pass by.
The death of gracious Queen Victoria caused much grief
Around the world, for she had held with strong belief
Those family ties which form a lasting bond for man,
Not only in the empire but in ev'ry land –
For interwoven with true and heartfelt sorrow
Were deep concerns for the world-without-her tomorrow.
Her role as head of a world empire gave her might
To will that continental thrones in peace unite.
In grief displaying loyalty that all understood,
Above all else she was perceived as being good –
As good as human frailties would humans allow:

Where would we ever find her gracious nature now?
In her long reign the railways spread across the world
Telecommunication cables far unfurled,
Whereby almost all great nations could fast converse,
With many other benefits that we can rehearse.
The telephone was also widespread, and a penny post
Throughout Britain was made available to most.
New Zealand then a separate colony became.
Fiji was next annexed by the empire, the same
Befell New Guinea which was one more of many
The empire took. To the East African company
A trade charter was granted, and as she reigned
Victoria, Empress of India was loud proclaimed.
And Jews in parliament were first allowed to sit,
The great wealthy Rothschild was the first to honour it.
All transportation of the convicts made to end:
Such wretches to far distant lands we'd no more send.
Among the engineering feats that still astound,
The Manchester Canal and Forth Bridge are renown.
In restless France a new republic they proclaim;
Until his end Napoleon III, robbed of his claim,
At Chislehurst in England spent his sad exile,
While the North-West Frontier Gay Gordon made safe in
    style.


## Edward VII

Edward the VII at last ascends the throne as king
And to the age an elegance of spirit bring.
His first unhappy duty was to bring the queen
From Osborne House in which her last short stay had been.
A convoy of warships escorted her corpse by sea:

124

A military state funeral there was to be.
Through London Town a throng of thousands strong sad crowd
And, following the cortège, rode the Kaiser proud.
Next rode the kings of Belgium and of Portugal
With heads of other nations, grieving one and all.
After an impressive service, by Windsor's Keep
Beside her beloved consort she was laid to sleep:
Together now for evermore in restful peace,
In Frogmore mausoleum where her grief could cease.
Beside Albert thus she laid her sovereign head
And both ennoble now the kingdom of the dead.
After the funeral the Kaiser stayed awhile
A warm ovation would ensure he left in style.
In pomp and grandeur King Edward in splendour rode
To open parliament, that wise and great abode.
And after he journeyed on to Hamburg, to sister's bed,
Where she in illness laid her ailing, regal head.
Meanwhile came the Duke and Duchess of Cornwall's
    world tour:
Six months of arduous travel they with pride endure,
Visiting far-flung corners of our empire spread wide,
The pair were most welcomely greeted on every side.
They stayed at Aden, India, Ceylon, Gibraltar,
New Zealand, Canada, Australia and Malta –
So many of the British possessions abroad
Which we had won o'er time by trade and by the sword.
A most enthusiastic welcome met them when home
From fifty thousand miles of world they tireless roam,
Which ever closer bound the empire in goodwill
And raised the status of the crown yet higher still.
During this tour the duke opened for Britain's king
A parliament for Australia, from which would spring
A newly created Commonwealth of world renown

Which still a true allegiance gave to England's crown.
The High Commissioner of South Africa came
To London to receive its freedom and acclaim.
Lord Roberts, too, returned to England having won
Great battles in the Boer War, and so begun
An end to that disastrous fight where none would yield.
He first reorganised the army in the field,
Both Kimberley and Ladysmith from siege relieved
And, as onwards his victorious men slowly weaved,
He took Bloemfontein and Pretoria from the foe
And with bit between his teeth would not let go.
He captured their General Gronje, annexed Transvaal
And Orange River colonies, and then set sail
To be with honour and delight at home received
While the king through parliament a vast sum to him
    bequeathed.
Three thousand men who served in that horrific war
Along Horseguards Parade they marched the king before,
Proudly wearing the medals they so well deserved,
A token of gratitude from those they served.
By the treaty of Vereeniging there ended
The Second Boer War, most bitterly contended.
The Duke of Cornwall was restyled the Prince of Wales
For all his wide-flung travels and his loyal travails.
A coronation at Westminster Abbey won
With ceremony the hearts and minds of everyone.
A magnificent procession was planned that day,
With crowds of cheering subjects waving along the way,
Then would come the Abbey's solemn but splendid rite.
Alas, the king was taken ill with pain that night,
So no procession through London as planned took place.
The king from surgery recovered with good grace
Postponed festivities belatedly went ahead

With all relieved that good King Edward was not dead!
With no grand procession, and a shorter service held,
But otherwise all pomp and circumstance unfurled.
Six thousand great and good attend this huge affair,
Representatives from the colonies were there.
Edward, Osborne House gave to the nation as a gift
For use to convalesce the badly wounded if
And when in future bloody wars the need arose.
All round the world a welling tide of goodwill flows –
And even the German, French and Russian press
Heartfelt best wishes to Edward they freely express.
The States, too, treated the coronation as their own
And in their delighted enthusiasm were not alone,
For even China and Japan joined the world acclaim
To wish the king a well and prosperous long reign.
The public pageant, postponed when the king fell ill,
Had taken place to much relief and great goodwill,
Many foreign state heads already had returned.
The king so much his people's devotion had earned
That they rejoiced that he was now once more in health:
Such loyal love is worth far more than fame or wealth!
Here at St Paul's thanksgiving services were held
As all those fears that he might die were now dispelled.
Next year a grand Durbar at Delhi was devised
Where Edward as emperor formally recognised.
As Indian princes and chieftains homage paid to him,
He, the hearts and minds of his vast empire sought to win.
This festival would last for days with grand review
As native troops and British troops proceeded to
Parade before the king, who sat upon a throne
And it seemed the imperial rule was set in changeless stone.
Not long before a Mad Mullah an army raised
In African Somaliland, with power crazed,

Against the British Abyssinian peaceful lands
With raiding and looting by his warrior bands.
At first he beat the British forces many times:
It seemed as if he would achieve his grand designs.
But he had not the lesson learnt that Englishmen
Admit not to defeat, but fight and fight again,
Whate'er the odds against, whate'er the pain.
He was defeated in the year 1904,
A treaty signed, pushed back to where he was before.
Trade terms were by Britain, China and high Tibet
Revised as they proved neither good nor fair as yet,
And boundaries between Tibet and India were also drawn,
O'er which too many disputes in the past were born.
The unwise Tibetans procrastinated too long;
British troops marched into Tibet to right that wrong,
Colonel Younghusband's planned intent to treat with each
Country's Amban and Llama 'til terms they reach.
At first no serious opposition rose as yet
Until unruly Tibetan soldiers they met
Who, well equipped, a frantic, wild attack began.
They with great loss of life were beaten to a man.
More skirmishes and fights slowed up the progress made
Until the capital Lhasa before them laid.
Here terms of lasting peace were arranged amicably:
Future disputes by negotiation would settled be.
A war between Japan and Russia had begun,
For Russia had Manchuria previously overrun.
Instead of withdrawing her encamped troops as pledged,
Designs on Korean ports, Russia created a wedge
Which threatened the adjoining Japanese state:
Alarmed, Japan would not accept this unsafe fate.
The Russians claimed it was to protect the Chinese and
The Trans-Siberian Railway that criss-crossed their land.

In spite of long negotiations no Russians would go,
No other choice was left: Japan the war must go.
Britain and all the other powers neutral stayed,
But often Russia this neutrality betrayed
By seizing British merchantmen and foreign ships.
They had to apologise for these atrocious 'slips'
And compensation paid to make partial redress,
Which did not Great Britain for long atone or impress.
Shortly after, when the Russian fleet made way
To Manchuria's long siege, they chose to spray
An English fishing fleet – as it unarmed did trawl –
With cannon shot, an act which would England appal.
We mobilised our deadly fleet to join the fray
And make the Russians rue the actions of that day.
But fortunately a concord reached in Paris meant
The Russians for their hostile actions could repent.
Once more a sum of compensation to us came
When all concurred the Russians clearly were to blame.
An Anglo-Japanese defence alliance was signed,
Securing peace in Asia with our rights defined,
And well the Chinese and the Indian borders keep
Against aggressors who might with armies sweep:
When faced with powers pledged to come to mutual aid,
Such ambitions of would-be attackers were stayed.
The Duke of Connaught on the king's behalf set forth
To Egypt, Ceylon and the Straits where every wharf
Was thronged by excited greeting crowds and official pride
When through these colonies he in processions ride.
The king had in the past already travelled wide
And so well knew his colonies from every side.
He saw the need for royalty to keep in sight
The splendour and the pomp of his imperial might.
Those travels too gave him sound knowledge of each land

And helped him their special needs to understand.
Edward was educated well for future rule
And often made worldwide travels a life-long school.
He visited Canada and America when young
And charmed the crowds who on his every word hung.
And when his father the Prince Consort sadly died,
With grief his health ebbed and he could not reside
Where memories of happier times would cloud his mind,
He left for Egypt and the Holy Land, to find
Recuperation from ill-health and sorrow's pain:
No British prince since Edward I had that terrain
And Holy Land visit made, but Edward, bereaved, so chose –
With what mixed feelings of joy and grief, who knows?
On returning home, he married amid much glee
His Princess Alexandria, who would faithful be.
He lived a country gentleman's unruffled life,
Journeyed through Ireland and Europe, where Crimean strife
On battlefields had lately left their baleful trace
Which proved the English were not an invincible race.
In here may lie the feelings he long held for peace,
A strong desire that all such bloody wars should cease.
When he fell ill with typhoid fever, then got well,
St Paul's a service held and rang its grateful bell.
Three hundred persons this happy service attend,
Delighted that this dire disease should so well end.
Had not Prince Albert died from this dreadful disease?
So Edward's full recovery could not but please.
He visited India where loyalty was shown,
He deputised for the ageing queen alone,
Playing a central role in both her Jubilees,
And burdens of office, from her last years he frees.
King Edward pursued always policies of peace,
That endless bickering across Europe should cease.

He toured Vienna, Paris, Rome and Naples, where
Enthusiastic goodwill and welcome he met there.
He met most royal heads and president of France
Where the Entente Cordiale his skilful charms advance.
All differences between Britain and France would be
Now settled in a spirit of calm amity.
While similar treaties with other powerful states
Were signed, and old mistrust and strife he thus abates.
Peacemaker Edward on the world scene left his mark:
Towards the goal of peace he steered the war-torn ark.
No doubt a true desire for peace informed his plan,
But just how vulnerable defending distant land!
The Boer War had taught this bitter lesson well:
How long the empire could be held, no one could tell.
Superior arms had helped to spread the flag so wide,
But could not be long held if arms equipped each side
Which enemies of our state to such opposition supplied.
By force of arms alone, could freedoms be denied?
The sun of empire seemed to some to near its end,
For law and order on it many still depend.
Edward relished his life and gave his reign a charm
Of elegance and joie de vivre which caused no harm.
His health grew poor, so to Biarritz he went in spring,
But this turned out to be a tragic, unwise thing.
The March of 1910 was unseasonably cold
And our beloved king was very ill and old.
He caught a severe chill, but he made light of it,
Returned to England where, although still far from fit,
He made inspection of the Sandringham Estate
In weather cold and wet, which surely sealed his fate.
Severely ill, he then succumbed and sadly died
With all the grieving royal family by his side.
After lying in state he was to Windsor Castle borne,

As all the heads of Europe and his people mourn.
No monarch's death was by so many keenly felt.
Beside his tomb the Spirit of World Peace weeping knelt.


## George V

George Frederick the Prince of Wales became our king
With all the pomp and circumstance, a noble thing
Which long traditions of state had shown to be
An outward sign of command and dignity
That gives a focus for the people's love of style,
Lifting them out of their mundane cares for a while,
Making them proud to be subjects of such a realm
With such colourful royalty there at its helm.
Just like the rites of church, these ceremonies inspire:
Of pomp and circumstance the people never tire.
A fishing rights dispute between the United States
And England was sent to The Hague for just debates,
Which reached agreement to Canada's grateful joy:
Newfoundland folk could now their fishing fleets employ
Without the risk of harassment or naval war!
If only arbitration could become firm law
Between all countries in this restless, troubled world,
Mankind might not into wasteful wars be hurled!
The Anglo-Japanese alliance was renewed;
Here the powers of the House of Lords were wide reviewed,
By which the Lords could not the Commons' will oppose,
Which after due debate enacts the laws it chose.
The coronation of the king was celebrated
With all due pomp and circumstance as he was fêted
By loyal crowds who lined the processional way,
With heads of colonies and princes on display.

Their Majesties at Spithead next reviewed the fleet
With some two hundred warships sailing them to greet.
Then came Prince Edward's investiture by the king
Within Caernavon Castle, which to the Welsh would bring
A source of pride and recognition by the crown,
Which by tradition has to the eldest son come down.
Now falls the blow that will echo around the world:
Into the chaos of world war all states are hurled.
Austria's admired archduke a single gunshot slays
As Serbian separatists set all Europe ablaze.
First Austria war on Serbia vows, then Russia tries
'All on behalf of Slavs' her troops to mobilise.
This gives the Germans good excuse her army vast
To mobilise for action and conquest at last,
For nothing harms an army more than idle hands
Just itching to reconquer the rich surrounding lands.
The dogs of war when once from all restraint set free
Would seldom let their weaker helpless victims flee.
Now Germany against the French through neutral Belgium
    press;
Great Britain, to defend the Belgians, joins in the mess.
Soon all the world joins in the struggle which will close
Old regimes already suffering their last feeble throes:
For all the ceremonies and pomp could never hide
The rottenness of deep, unjust distress inside,
And in a few short years they all vanish from sight:
For a short while the world is plunged into cold night.
Meanwhile the armies engaged in senseless slaughter;
Only unrest and famine made the Germans falter.
In May of 1919* the Great World War was won,

---

*Following the Armistice of November 1918, the final peace treaty terms were presented to the German plenipotentiaries on May 7th 1919.

But now the cause of future conflicts had begun.
The beaten Germans ceded Alsace Lorraine to France
And large repayments to the victors sapped their finance;
She lost the valued colonies she held overseas:
With much restricted armed forces, she was on her knees.
The aftermath of war its deadly harvest reaps
As many monarchs by hungry mobs were cast on heaps:
Republics grew apace and ancient dynasties
Like leaves before the winds of history fast flees.
Once men mount the throne to rule for country's good,
They are obliged to succeed, tis understood –
But if they fail the peace and wealth to well maintain,
They lose the privilege and right to rule again.
In Russia, badly beaten by German might,
An angry mob the ruling class and Tsar now fight:
The Tsar and all his family were put to death
And of the ancient Russian empire naught was left.
The shock of regicide sent shudders through those kings
Who feebly to their royal privilege still clings.
He who would raise the wind oft reaps the hurricane.
The winning powers let the Communists attain
Control in the false hope old Russia to destroy,
But Russia never would fall victim to this ploy.
She beat the loyalists, the Whites' attacks repelled,
Against all odds her armies, inspired by hope, excelled
To form the first all-Communist government –
Of which the world outside would learn to long repent.
Some of its former states achieved self-rule,
So weakening the Russian state, which did not fall.
The Kaiser fled exiled to Holland's fertile land;
The Austro-Hungarian empire too would disband.
A new republic of Poland was first created,
Whose birth in troubled times to troubled times was fated.

At home a People's Act gave more the right to vote:
Against autocratic rule another blow was smote.
For women, too, the right to vote for some was given:
In the Great War they had so heroically striven.
In troubled Ireland, too, was formed the new Sinn Fein
Which fought so hard an independent state to gain.
Only the Northern parts remained a loyal friend
On which alone the British could at least depend.
Nor must we view Sinn Fein's motives in such bad light:
If we were held unfree by force, would we not fight?
In order to appease the government, the two divide
And give a 'parliament' of sorts to either side.
A council of Ireland entire was formed to aid
Much better feelings and a foundation laid
For but one parliament to govern all Ireland,
But this only increased Sinn Fein's self-rule demand.
And under De Valera Sinn Fein waged a war
Of violent destruction not seen before,
From assassinations, ambushes and great bloodshed:
It seemed as if the whole of troubled Ireland bled.
A conference could not agree the terms for peace
As De Valera his obstruction would not cease.
So he in time by Michael Collins was replaced,
Who soon agreements reached, but some held he disgraced
The hard Sinn Fein's extremists' long-fought cause
Who wished to murder, bomb and destroy without a pause.
They would not ratify the terms by him agreed;
They would fight on until the whole of Ireland freed.
A civil war erupted which Collins army won
When they the Dublin Courts attacked with lethal gun.
The rebel army melted into remote small bands,
But still opposed the terms agreed with hostile plans.
Then they ambushed the 'traitor' Collins, whom they killed,

Who had so many of their aspirations filled,
For Southern Ireland now became the Irish Free State
(Appeasement never shuts aggression's kicked-in gate),
A dominion within the British empire's sphere –
A compromise which much bloodshed had bought so dear.
The tomb of Tutankhamun by the English was found,
Whose famous treasures would the whole world astound.
Who could not look upon the Pharaoh's golden face
And not marvel at such serene and youthful grace?
With social change came first Labour's chance to rule,
But soon they had their hands with countless troubles full.
The widespread General Strike of 1924
Was by the force of state suppressed, but not before
It showed the power that in striking workers lay
Who would not for their justified cause accept delay.
Sir Malcolm Campbell's 'Bluebird' reached record speed,
A triumph of his and England's engineers indeed!
Broadcasts and television were at an early stage:
Who could foretell the social changes they'd presage?
A fatal flu the reaper's scythe more coffins fill,
As if to mock the hubris of man's boasted skill.
For half a million was the first state pension paid,
A giant step towards social justice this made!
A woman as a cabinet minister stood,
Which could only be for the country's long-term good.
The useful telephone service became widespread
And speech across a shrinking world still faster sped.
Then Britain felt the greatest, most violent earthquake,
Whose tremors from the south to Scotland north did shake.
Lone Winston Churchill warned: 'Defenceless are we now',
Which with a growing threat of war none should allow.
Ramsay MacDonald wouldn't the hunger marchers meet,
Which most of Labour's moral principles defeat:

136

For when the reins of government on Labour fall,
They found they governed not for loyal few, but all.
In 1935 the Silver Jubilee
Of king and queen was celebrated with great glee.
Alas next year the king's untimely death all mourn –
A more unsettled age after his death was born.


## Edward VIII

Edward VIII assumed the ancient role of king,
But with his love affair our country's woes soon bring.
He would not rule without his lady at his side,
But she, as divorcee, the state could not abide.
Therefore King Edward decides his throne to abdicate,
Leaving his brother reluctant to face his fate.
Edward to France in exile sailed with his true love –
Yet kings, 'twas thought, should place their duty high above
Their personal wishes, which privilege entails,
And he who walks away from this his people fails.
A popular and well-loved prince made things much worse
He, just before his empire, put his own needs first.
What has been widely thought and said should well suffice,
For in the end 'twas he who made his sacrifice.
He was no coward, who to pressure did not give in:
For that, if little else, some praise is due to him.
Cool reason cannot understand how deep love binds,
For love has ever baffled the cleverest of minds.

# George VI

By fate thrust forth, King George ascends the shaken throne
With modesty and quiet calm – and not alone:
He with his wife and children calms the ruffled state
And once again the British throne is seen as great.
When a royalty can to its people standards give
And in a decent family circle loving live,
Unrest abroad and colonial upsets prevent
His reign from rest and peace nor know a calm content.
When Adolf Hitler chose in 1938
To march on Vienna, he gambled with fate,
Yet none of the Great Powers with force intervenes
Though Chamberlain with him appeasing talks convenes.
The memory of slaughter in the First World War
Made Chamberlain all thought of armed conflict abhor.
Instead by calming talks he seemed concord to reach:
'Peace in our time' he claimed – until there came the breach
When Hitler occupied Sudetenland in scorn
A terrible evil across the whole of Europe was born.
Into Moravia and Bohemia the Germans strut
And into pieces all peace treaties cut.
Over 1939 the clouds of war descend
And 'all the lights went out' and joys of peace have end.
'Hands off Poland!' Great Britain now demands at last,
But Hitler still invaded Poland with Blitzkrieg fast
That swept aside the brave, out-gunned resisting Pole –
Across their borders Panzer troops swift roll.
So Chamberlain forced to declare a fatal war:
No one could trust the Führer's pledges any more.
In Germany this evil tyrant commands that state,
Attacked weak nations with uncompromising hate.
Who one by one before his Blitzkrieg succumb;

Most shaken by his strength of will, the world was dumb.
Great Powers passively stood by as dogs of war
Savaged the ancient states, destroying all before
With pitiless, inhuman and brutal force of might
That cast the whole of Europe in dreadful night.
Denmark and Norway were next to be invaded:
Our blood, our sweat and tears could not be evaded.
Once Germany attacked Poland the die was cast:
We could not let these friends, unhelped, fall fast.
An ultimatum to withdraw the fiends ignore
And with heavy heart we mobilised our troops for war.
Had not poor Chamberlain fought hard to keep the peace,
But Adolf Hitler would not his acts of conquest cease.
He signed a worthless pact for peace in this our time,
Then went ahead to implement his brutal crime.
Though Chamberlain was oft derided, he won delay
And preparations were made against a feared-for day.
The slaughter of the First World War was fresh in mind,
No one to all the waste of warfare could be blind.
Alas, when France capitulates their foe before,
Alone England would face his wrath from nearby shore.
With much of Europe 'neath his onward-marching feet,
The Führer bragged the British he would soon defeat.
And when in triumph he o'er Paris looked with scorn,
Invasion plans on England's island home were born.
No state so far the fury of his Blitzkrieg felt
Without great loss of nerve and before him knelt,
Submitting to his harsh demands with undue haste
As his brute armies laid the beaten states to waste.
How great the prize if England were to now submit
And Hitler o'er its empire vast could run his writ!
Would not the conquest of the world be in his grasp?
The British troops in France, retreating, could not last;

When at Dunkirk were driven back towards the sea,
Where they had nowhere else to fight, or hide, or flee.
When Winston Churchill feared his army could be lost
He knew he had to get them back whate'er the cost.
And all our little ships responded to his call
To help the exposed army to these shores recall.
The 'miracle' of Dunkirk delivered our men
To rest at home awhile, then fight the foe again.
The Battle of Britain thus began not on the sea,
Where England's naval might forbade, keeping the Channel
    free,
But from the open heights of unprotected air
That would, they hoped, reduce England to deep despair.
By night and day an armada of German planes
Like angry wasps swarmed in, in spiteful stinging lanes
To bomb old England 'til they bowed before such might
As homes and factories in flames lit up each night.
Against them rose the gallant Spitfires of the few,
Undaunted by the overwhelming force – they knew
Each sortie meant a dance with death in autumn skies.
In such brave hands the fate of battered England lies.
'Ne'er was so much owed by so many to so few,'
Said Churchill in just praise of each air fighter crew.
The Battle of Britain was won by these undaunted brave,
Who boldly fought our threatened isle to timely save.
Meanwhile, Churchill commanded the navy to destroy
The fleet of France lest it the Germans should deploy
In fresh invasion plans, or use to help blockade
Our island home which sore depends on foreign trade.
Tough choices total war demands just to survive,
For neither side old moral values keep alive.
No other state his savage Blitzkreig could withstand
And let the Stormtroopers jackboot across their land –

But once the Battle of Britain was soundly lost,
With many planes and pilots so completely lost,
Herr Hitler his invasion dream had to defer:
Britain, he thought, could not his wider scheme deter.
He carried on his bombing raids with spiteful hate,
But lost his chance and left his prize until too late.
So many thought old England could not long withstand
The constant bombing of its ancient cities grand,
But they and Hitler failed to heed the stubborn will
That takes each blow upon the chin and fights on still.
The more the pain inflicted, the more our spirits grew:
We'd fight and not surrender 'til we had won through.
Amidst the smouldering rubble of a bombed-out street,
A kneeling woman scrubs her doorstep spruce and neat.
Such was the stoic pride and guts of common folk
Who wouldn't by the devastating Blitz be broke.
Like hounds denied the prize of hunted easy bait,
The dogs of war unleashed cannot be made to wait.
So Hitler turned them round and Russia soon invaded
With rapid speed and through the steppes in bloodshed waded.
The startled Russian troops did in disarray recede
As fast his Panzer columns swept through at breakneck speed,
Annexing vast and boundless tracts of Russian soil,
O'er burnt-out crops where neither food was left nor oil.
And long and thin their lines of vital supplies came,
Yet if they could but take Moscow they'd win the game.
Old Stalin, like some grim, ferocious, brown bear –
Supported by British convoys – stood fast, confronting there
The German jackals circling round his city walls
And on his men 'take arms and fight to death' he calls.
Next came the harsh, cold winds of winter's savage chill
And Hitler's swift advance came to an icy still.
At first they tried to force their way with bitter fight,

141

But in the end before those winter blasts took flight.
They straggled slowly back in terrible defeat
With feet of ice, bowed before fierce driving sleet.
The harsh lessons of history all men ignore:
Was not this too the fate of Bonaparte before?
Yet hubris clouds the vaunting mind – believes it can
Outdo the failing efforts made by previous man.
And so the tide of war began to slowly turn:
Oh, when will man the wastefulness of war relearn?
America came late onto the tragic scene,
For Europe's war was not their cause to intervene –
'Til Japan Pearl Harbor bombed their helpless fleet,
The US entered the war and helped defeat
The German might and then against Japan they fought,
But every victory was most dearly bought.
Yet when they came in force all knew the war was won,
And so the great advance on Germany had begun.
Montgomery for Britain Rommel's army beat
At Alamein, that led to his complete defeat.
First through the desert depths, then up through Italy's toe,
The Allies fought the still-resisting, well-armed foe.
Next came the vast invasion of Europe's shore
As from old England warships began to pour.
The Germans fought most bravely until their end,
Against the vengeful Russians their own homes defend.
Meanwhile, the Führer in his bunker would not give in –
He fantasised that with just one more blow he'd win.
Then, with the Russians at the door, he knew his fate
And shot himself, evading capture and the hate
Of Russian vengeful spite with Roman stoic pride:
He, his own destiny, own death, alone would decide.
His all-consuming will is what we most admire,
Albeit turned to evil ends and means most dire.

142

No one can e'er forgive the gassing of the Jew,
Nor the fatal reign of death which across the world he threw.
Had not a Golden Age with dreams of good to come
Beneath this tyrant's troop to gory waste succumb?
The war in Europe at last reached its weary end,
But still the Japs their conquests zealously defend.
US on Hiroshima, Nagasaki dropped
The first atomic bombs – all fighting stopped.
An awful power lay in mankind's treach'rous hands,
Its mushroom clouds cast shadows o'er all lands.
Pandora's deadly box once more was opened wide
And none could thrust its dreadful evils back inside.
Exhausted England reaped the aftermath of war,
No longer was as rich and robust as it was before.
So slowly from her empire she had to withdraw,
No longer could she rule or other nations o'erawe.
Perhaps the Führer helped in unintended ways
To bring to its demise the hour of empire days.
Nothing becomes a nation more, accepting change,
With which great style a handing-over can arrange
Of independence to their former colonies
Instead of holding vainly on 'til all strength flees.
For all the world had changed and once-proud imperial
    might
Was thought in this new post-war age no longer right.
Although it was within its time a worthy aim,
The changing world held colonising in great shame.
But in its hour our empire was the greatest known,
Policied the world and many benefits had sown:
The rule of law, democracy and fair play
Had for a golden age across vast lands held sway.
There was, also, a darker and more ruthless side,
But overall we can look back with proper pride.

143

King George VI went weary to his restful grave,
A man thrust into awful times yet quietly brave.

*The ancient scholar paused and stared into the night,*
*As if he saw some things beyond his present sight:*
And here I must this saga bring to a close,
Though England's genius in other realms now grows.
For people of such enterprise which they possess
Will never on their laurels past long rest,
But shall again create a future bright and fair
With values and visions for all mankind to share.
In other fields of excellence they shall prove their worth,
Add to the glory and splendour of this earth.
Whate'er their human faults, which are manifold,
They showed great enterprise, magnificent and bold.


## Epilogue

*Quo vadis?* Noble England, in this brave new world,
Through troubles, we have unbowed been hurled.
There are fresh fields to conquer, other foes to fight,
The plagues of strife, great poverty, to cure outright,
Deadly disease destroys the life of humankind:
Which we could overcome with heart and will and mind.